From client to individual . . .

Rose's Story

By Rose,
A Survivor of Our Social Services

Family Service America

Copyright 1991
Family Service America
11700 West Lake Park Drive
Milwaukee, Wisconsin 53224

Library of Congress Cataloging-in-Publication Data

Rose, a Survivor of Our Social Services, 1943–
        Rose's story / by Rose, a Survivor of Our Social Services.
        p.   cm.
        ISBN 0-87304-244-1
        1. Rose, a Survivor of Our Social Services, 1943–   . 2. Welfare
recipients—United States—Biography. 3. Foster children—United
States—Biography. 4. Adult children of dysfunctional families—
United States—Biography. 5. Mentally ill—United States—Biography.
6. Social service—United States—Case studies.
I. Family Service America. II. Title.
HV91.R67   1991
362.2'092—dc20   91–33602
|B|

Printed in the United States

Contents

Foreword

"Active listening," "accurate empathy," and "starting where the client is" are precepts in the social work profession. However, the profession's literature presents relatively few opportunities to "hear" what clients are saying, including their versions of what "being helped" is really like. *Rose's Story* tells us exactly what it was like from one client's perspective. Straightforward and uncluttered by sentiment or apparent motive, her story is a personal travelogue of a journey through the backwoods of our social welfare system.

A couple of texts—Yalom's *Every Day a Little Closer* and Fibush's *Forgive Me No Longer*—have attempted to shed light on what it's like to be on the receiving end of our helping systems. But these useful and revealing books cover the parallel and often contrapuntal accounts of therapist and client and are edited by the particular therapist. Tidied up as they are by the hindsight wisdom of the therapist/author, these books are helpful and instructive, providing the reader with a vicarious understanding of the therapeutic event as he or she is escorted through the human drama called therapy.

Rose's uncompromising chronicle offers few of these amenities. As she might say, "I'm just telling it like it is." Thus, readers find themselves involved in a private dialogue with Rose, trying to make sense of her life within the subjective framework of Rose's perception of it. Apart from complying with her social worker's request, Rose does not tell us why she wrote this account of her life; for that matter, we don't have any clue why her social worker asked her to write it. Her story is unprocessed and unrefined.

The accessible yet stark and unadorned prose of Rose's story marks this book as a valuable contribution to social work practice and education. Rose, in important ways, is every client—the client who may be entering or leaving a social worker's office or meeting a worker for the first time on her doorstep. Although clients' narratives may differ with regard to specific events and plot, they are likely to be just as raw and uneven as Rose's. In reading Rose, the reader/social worker is placed in the worker's chair, forced to listen actively to find sense, meaning, and purpose in what he or she is being told. *Rose's Story* is the next best thing to a face-to-face encounter with a client.

As such, this small volume is a useful companion to, if not an antidote for, the necessary abstractions of theory, systems, and practice methods found in textbooks. The latter deal with ideals of practice; Rose confronts the reality of practice. The "real" involves more than merely the primary relationship between the client and the worker: the system itself serves as an "actor" that may contaminate even the best intentions of the worker. In a moderate voice, without malice or reproval, Rose speaks of her many experiences with callous and insensitive social welfare professionals and, as well, with professionals who listened, cared, and made a difference in her life. Her account reveals breaches of social justice, personal rights, and ethical responsibility, in addition to self-serving policies, protocols, and rules that serve the system but not the needs of the client. Her account also tells us (indirectly, to be sure) how "good" services can help. To become an effective practitioner, one must learn the system in which services are rendered. Rose, it is safe to say, speaks on behalf of many clients who fall through the cracks in our systems.

As fruitful and useful as this book is for professional education, or, for that matter, for workers who need to reflect on their practice, there are some risks connected with the way *Rose's Story* might be interpreted. At one extreme, one might be tempted to celebrate Rose as a heroine, an exceptional survivor of hardships and deprivations that, according to our developmental systems, traumatize if not devastate less exceptional souls. At the other extreme, some might regard Rose as a screen upon which they might project their knowledge of human psychopathology. In so doing, they might view Rose as a "textbook case" (a circumstance that occurred often enough in some of her collisions with mental health professionals) in that depressions and repressions, loss of memory, and other "psychological deficits" provide fertile ground for theory.

But to see her either as a singular heroine or as a mental patient upon whom theory can be hung like clothing on a mannequin demeans the usefulness of this book for practice education. Each of these perspectives focuses only on the more spectacular interludes of her life—the breakdowns, the suffering, the victories. Although these aspects of Rose's life deserve attention and certainly are intriguing, they do not acquaint us with the various and interrelated facets of Rose as a person.

Rather, the reader's task is to discover the strengths, aspirations, visions, and other inner forces that allowed Rose to move through and eventually overcome many hardships. These more subtle aspects of Rose's life are not readily discernible in the text; one must read between the lines of her description of life in foster homes, institutions, bureaucracies, and courts to find clues to Rose's survival. These clues are not typically found at the pinnacles of her experiences but rather in the ordinary, prosaic patterns of her daily life. Personal strength is found in the daily decisions, judgments, and choices one makes to pay bills, obtain work, provide care for one's children, and otherwise cope with the stresses and demands of living. Wise readers will appreciate the "pathologies" and "symptoms" that are penalties for a lonely or burdened life. But they will also search for the strengths that make that life worth living. Rose's vitality was supported by her natural wisdom, her caring and regard for others, her integrity, and perhaps guilelessness. No doubt, these qualities also prompted Rose's desire to eventually become a social worker herself.

Rose's search, as she put it, was for "a good, decent woman that I could learn to love and trust." She found this woman in Diane, the therapist who prompted Rose to write this autobiography in the first place. Perhaps one day we will be graced with Diane's story. Then we will have a complete picture of what "good helping" looks like.

Howard Goldstein
Professor Emeritus
Case Western Reserve University

Acknowledgment

Rose's story might have been lost except for the fact that it was brought to a Court Appointed Special Advocate (CASA) office by Rose's attorney. Betty Nafziger, a former English teacher and volunteer writer for CASA, developed the manuscript by researching and verifying the facts through records and interviews. Ms. Nafziger perceived the value of Rose's story in promoting understanding of individuals who are raised in and sometimes become trapped by the welfare system. Through her persistent efforts, the manuscript was submitted and eventually accepted for publication by Family Service America.

Introduction

The information disseminated through textbooks and journals is a necessary component in the education and ongoing professional development of social service workers. But it's easy to forget that beneath the abstractions of academia, the impersonal "clients" for whom programs, practice models, policies, and theories are developed, lies the individual human being whose story, though implied, is seldom fully told. Rose tells that story. If our textbooks and journals serve as aerial photographs from which we draw our professional bearings, this book provides us with a close-up shot at ground level. Rose is the flower in the valley, the tree in the forest, the individual in the system.

If I were a fiction editor asked to consider this manuscript for possible publication, I would reject it. In my letter to the author, I might say that the realism toward which this story surely aims does not work. The main character is one-dimensional. The tragic events of her life, though compelling, are ultimately not believable. A reader needs a measure of relief from tragedy, a door through which at least the possibility of redemption is glimpsed. But in this story the doors, for the most part, are not only closed, they are triple bolted. But life, as they say, is often stranger than fiction.

When Rose was 35 years old, a therapist asked her to write her "story." The therapist expected to receive a half-dozen pages describing her childhood. Rose gave her 167 handwritten pages. That story is reproduced here essentially in its original form, although some vocabulary, spelling, and grammatical changes as well as chapter divisions have been inserted to facilitate readability.

The narrative is confusing, disturbing, even incomprehensible in its unrelenting portrayal of our foster care and mental health systems. In order to help round out the reader's perspective and to avoid some of the confusion inherent in Rose's telling of her story, the following information was summarized from welfare and hospital records as well as from Rose's narrative.

Rose's father deserted his wife and their six children soon after Rose was born. Six months later Rose's sickly and impoverished mother placed the children with social services. After her parents' divorce was finalized, Rose was placed with her father and stepmother. At 18 months of age, Rose was described by a social services pediatrician as an "extremely frail, white, thin baby who had had pneumonia, chicken pox, measles, and whooping cough. I recommend that she receive especially good care, food, and love."

At age two, Rose's father and stepmother released Rose to social services, and she was placed in a foster home. The foster parents were overly protective of her, and Rose learned that illness brought attention. At age seven, she still needed to be rocked and given a bottle in the morning before school.

Seventeen children were being warehoused at this foster home, and some trouble with adolescent boys eventually caused the home to be closed. Rose states, "I went to school and some lady picked us up in a car. She had our clothes and Julia [Rose's sister] said we were never going back home to Mommy [the foster mother] because she was mean. I felt really sad and confused. I also felt like it was all my fault."

At the children's receiving center Rose met her real father and stepmother and learned for the first time that her foster parents were not her real mother and father. Her father and stepmother took Julia home but told Rose that they couldn't take her because she was "too little and too much trouble."

Between the ages of seven and eight, Rose was shuttled among four foster homes, spent time in the hospital for tonsillitis, underwent eye surgery (she was severely cross-eyed), and was sexually abused. At age eight she was placed in a foster home where she received good care and religious training, but when this foster family attempted to adopt her, Rose's father refused.

At age 10 Rose was placed in a church orphanage where her behavior soon became problematic. According to records, she began to lie and lived in an elaborate fantasy world. When the orphanage authorities determined that they could no longer handle her, she was committed to a state mental hospital and wrongly diagnosed as "probable juvenile schizophrenic," despite the fact that the admitting physician listed her neurological responses as within the normal range. The physician noted that she fantasized, imagining herself in a beautiful field overlooking a valley and a farm. She envisioned her mother but did not hear her voice or talk to her. The psychiatrist noted that she discussed things that would normally produce joy or sorrow in a flat, monotonous manner. (As an adult, Rose was rediagnosed as suffering from recurrent cyclic depression.)

At age 11, Rose was stripped and scrubbed with a group of demented women. Incoming patients waiting for a physical examination were seated in a hallway with only a towel to cover themselves while workers and others walked by. There were no cubicles in the bathrooms for privacy. Many of the staff were recent high school graduates. Pay was low. Although the institution maintained three adolescent units, the authorities determined that Rose would be safer on the women's ward due to her small physical stature and inability to get along with other children. Schooling consisted of an occasional visiting tutor and a ready supply of library books. She was given Thorazine injections. Rose states, "I just took whatever came my way."

At age 14, after spending two years in a mental institution where she learned to "cooperate," Rose was returned to the foster care system. At one foster home, the foster mother made Rose shave her pubic hair and the foster father sexually abused her. When Rose told her stepmother, her stepmother laughed and said she was going to be a tramp just like her real mother.

A high school gym teacher discovered the abuse and Rose was placed in yet another foster home, where she remained until she achieved independence. At this home, too, she was sexually abused by the foster parents' teenage son.

So went the first 18 years of Rose's life—and so go the first three chapters of Rose's autobiography. In the remaining chapters, Rose describes her adult years and her struggle to release herself and her own children from the systems that raised her.

Rose's story is that of a befuddled survivor of systems: familial, welfare, institutional. There isn't a touch of lyricism in her narrative. The tone is factual, monotonous—this happened, then this happened, then this happened. But despite this, or perhaps because of this, the story is compelling. The litany of facts and events lies like cellophane over a struggling child. Her emotional, psychological, and physical survival depends on her acceptance of the system, the only parent she knows. Like a character out of a Kafka novel, Rose learned to adapt to the system's capricious, often cruel demands.

To the layperson, Rose's autobiography may appear incomprehensible, even unbelievable, in places, although an experienced mental health worker has probably seen numerous variations of this story during his or her professional career. Foster parents, social workers, relatives, husbands, friends, physicians appear, disappear, and reappear like characters in a bad dream. For good or ill, they touch her life, then fade away. Their motivations are obscure and suspect, ominous within the context of Rose's vague perceptions of them. One wishes to ask why—why does Rose's sister dangle Rose by her feet outside a fourth-story window? Why does a foster mother poke Rose with pins and make her walk around the block wearing a diaper and a sign reading "I wet the bed"? Why do Rose's birth father and stepmother refuse to allow her to be adopted even though they will not allow her to live with them? Why was Rose committed to a state mental institution? Why do physicians contradict one another with diagnoses and medications? Why do social workers attempt to undermine her precarious mental and emotional stability by attempting to take away her children? Why did no one ask Rose to tell her story before she was 35 years old?

If the reader is searching for answers to these and the myriad other questions that arise from a reading of this book, he or she will be sorely disappointed. Answers appear in textbooks, not in autobiographies. Rose seldom speculates; she learned at a very young age that to ask why was to become vulnerable to further change and perhaps worse life conditions. Beneath Rose's litany of events lies the terrible silence of disconnection and dissolution. The gap between cause and effect is too wide. When a child is stripped and made to stand naked in a kitchen because she ate a hot lunch at school, she does not ask why. To do so is to become vulnerable to even more terrible and capricious answers. Rather, the child takes refuge in the silence of punishment, which at least is comprehensible on its own terms.

Rose's autobiography opens when she is four years old, the "first year and first foster home" she can remember. After briefly naming the other foster children in the home, she states, "Soon little Phyllis was taken away kicking and screaming by a welfare worker. I think she went back to her real mother. After this the family moved us all to a big farm in an area that was pretty isolated."

This event, like all of the events in Rose's story, is described simply, directly, exactly as a child might perceive it. But between a kicking and screaming child being carried away by a welfare worker and the move to a big farm in an isolated area lies silence. Time and logic are dissolved by the incongruity of Rose's description of a kicking, screaming child going back to her mother followed immediately by a move to a farm. The reader is left with two images: (1) a moving van loaded with the family's possessions and following the welfare worker and screaming child out the driveway (obviously false) and (2) a four-year-old child witnessing a frightening event, the meaning of which, even at 35 years of age, she is unable to comprehend and assimilate into the fabric of her own life. Both literally and figuratively, Rose moves on. But the reader is left with the disconcerting image of a child emotionally arrested by an incomprehensible life experience. Does she peek around the corner, thumb stuck like a pacifier in her mouth? Does she test her own precarious situation by tugging on her foster mother's dress and asking for a cookie? We will never know; perhaps Rose does not know.

Throughout this narrative, the reader must contend with all that Rose does not and cannot say. Although the events speak for themselves, they do not say nearly enough. The narrative not only raises questions about the motivations of the professionals who purport to help Rose, but about the "truthfulness" of Rose's descriptions of the events themselves. When I initially read Rose's story, I found myself, at times, becoming irritated with Rose, especially as the narrative moved into her adult years. I wished for her to question the callousness and insensitivity of those who "helped" her. I wanted her to tell her story to someone who would listen or, barring this, just once to stomp her foot and shake her fist at God. Her passive acceptance of the system's capricious demands caused me to question the veracity of her narrative as much as it did the motivations of the system. I felt disgusted with the systems that mistreated her, but irritated at Rose for acquiescing to this mistreatment.

A number of years ago a man, whose tongue was planted firmly in his check, told me, "If I had a new suit of clothes to give away, and a poor person wearing rags and a wealthy person wearing a $500 suit were standing in front of me, I'd probably give my suit of clothes to the wealthy person. He'd know how to wear them." Upon reflection, I realized that my irritation with Rose put me squarely in line with the systems with which I felt disgusted. Our systems serve as buffers that separate us from messy human needs. When they don't work, we blame the individual for not making them work. Instead of evaluating the relationship between the individual and the system, we dress our systems in even finer clothers, hoping that they will eventually be handed down to those who truly need them. What we conveniently forget is that the clothing is often worn and tattered by the time they receive it.

This book calls into question the relationship between the individual and the system. In evaluating the book for publication, I envisioned it as a teaching tool for undergraduate and graduate courses in social work. As an ancillary text, I felt it would be like bringing field work into the classroom. But because of the inconsistencies and contradictions in Rose's story, I also thought that the narrative needed commentary by a social services professional in order to elicit meaningful classroom discussion. To this end, we began searching for a social worker who might write an introduction and provide commentary on each chapter.

Upon first reading the manuscript, the reviewers to whom we sent the manuscript, without exception, were excited about its possibilities. "Yes," this story needed to be told, and "yes," a commentary would be useful for classroom discussion. But when they returned to the manuscript to draw out comments and professional issues that might elicit discussion, they were blocked. Invariably, they still saw the value of Rose's story but they had difficulty devising a meaningful, chapter-by-chapter commentary.

The responses of these reviewers, I believe, reflect the dilemmas inherent in the education and training of social services professionals. As Howard Goldstein (1991) states,

> *Conventional wisdom has it that there is a "continuum" or "dialectic" or some kind of resonance between theory and practice . . . progress in practice will be the payoff for progress in theory development. . . . My students obediently confirmed this premise by their active note taking in the classroom. But on observing them and conversing with them in the field . . . it became difficult . . . to ignore the hard evidence that what they were doing in practice didn't seem to depend on the enlightenment my classroom theories provided.*

Rose's autobiography and the reactions of professionals who attempted to comment on it highlight the conflict between theory and practice, system and individual. The individual's story is always open ended, amorphous. To attempt to contain it within the intellectual and functional parameters of theory and system is like trying to hold water in a porous container. Goldstein goes on to say, "Practice should inform theory, not the other way around." And to take Goldstein's observation one step further, the individual's story should inform the systems within which so many vulnerable individuals are floundering. In the final analysis, the accuracy of the facts is secondary to the individual's perception of them.

The inability of these professionals to deliver a commentary is not to suggest that this book is irrelevant to the classroom experience. On the contrary, it suggests, I believe, that such a commentary pales within the context of Rose's life experience. Her story deserves to stand alone, to serve as the place from which textbook theory and classroom discussion begin, not end.

For 35 years, Rose's life was condensed and compartmentalized to fit the neatly ruled boxes of forms and reports. Although one-word labels and single-paragraph summaries may be great for record-keeping procedures, they don't do much for the self-esteem of individuals who sense, despite their life experience, that they might be worth more. Hence, 167 handwritten pages when someone finally bothers to ask, "What's your side of the story?"

Rose's life serves as testimony to the individual's ability to survive, while simultaneously serving as a mirror to the potential contradictions and vanity of our human service systems. Theories, research, and practice models can't hide the wrinkles and warts of our systems when we fail first to listen to the individual's story. Although this autobiography may preclude a formal commentary, it should, after self-righteousness and indignation are stripped away, stimulate heated and beneficial classroom discussion. The mirror seldom shows us what we want to see. Read on.

Robert Nordstrom
Senior Editor
Families in Society
The Journal of Contemporary
Human Services

Note

Goldstein, H. (1992). If it hasn't made progress as a science, might social work be an art? *Families in Society, 73* (1).

Childhood

1

Dear Diane,

I am writing this as best as I can remember. As we know from records, I was born June 15, 1943. The first year and the first foster home I can remember was in 1947.

I was living with a family, an older couple by the name of Jim and Ruth Cooper. The home was on Plum Street in Waterford, Ohio. In the home besides myself were other foster children, two of whom were my two older real sisters, Julia and Annette. There was a girl, Maxine, about Annette's age, 11 years old, and a little girl, Phyllis, who was about 3 years old.

Soon little Phyllis was taken away kicking and screaming by a welfare worker. I think she went back to her real mother. After this the family moved us all to a big farm in an area that was pretty isolated.

The husband was a troubleshooter for a trucking company and was gone quite a lot. After we moved to the farm they got two other children, Bobby and Beth, who were twins age seven.

Despite all the children in the home, the only real uproars and arguments were always centered around Julia. She was usually lying and stealing at home and from her teachers in school. She hated me with a passion and was always deliberately hurting me every chance she got. If I had to go to the field with her, she would always end up beating me with a tobacco stick. She would blow her nose on my dresstail every chance she got, so I would get a spanking. They had a huge dog, and when she fed it, she would try to make it bite me, because it was mean and kept tied up. One time Mrs. Cooper caught her doing it and yelled at her. Julia got so angry with me, she slammed the screen door on my foot deliberately and tore my heel off on the tin strip. I still have a big scar from where the doctor had to sew the heel back. After that, matters only got worse between us. The rest of the family and I got along very well.

The year of 1948 I started kindergarten in Waterford. At this time we all moved again back into Waterford next to the American Legion Hall.

Julia's abuse continued even at school. However, when I started the first grade my teacher picked up on this because of bruises I had constantly, along with other children in Julia's class telling her of things she was doing to hurt me on the playground.

When my teacher asked me about it, I was terrified, because no matter what Julia did to me I never told anyone because she said if I did they would put her in prison and beat her and give her only bread and water. Considering my age, I believed her, and I loved her because she was my sister and didn't ever want anything to happen to her.

About a week later I went to school and some lady picked us up in a car. She had our clothes and Julia said we were never going back home to Mommy because she was mean. I felt really sad and confused. I also felt like it was all my fault that my teacher found out.

I didn't know Julia had lied to the welfare and told them that she was the one being abused by the foster parents. She certainly reversed everything, telling them I was a sick little girl who lied on her, and they believed her without ever asking me anything.

The worker took us straight to the Children's Receiving Center that day. When we got there, Annette and I were crying. However, Julia was as happy as a lark.

As if the day's events weren't enough of a shock, Julia immediately began handing out my clothes and dolls to the other kids. My protests meant nothing to anyone as they were busy checking in five new kids. She then said that as long as we both lived I would never have anything I loved again if she was around. I have to admit I was a little relieved when I was separated from her and the others from the foster home because of my age.

Childhood

A matron gave me a real shock when for the first time I learned that the Coopers were not my real mommy and daddy. Later that month I met my real dad and my stepmother for the first time I remember. It was an odd meeting when this strong man and woman came in carrying a doll as big as me. My stepmother said she was my mother and she loved me but Julia had had such a hard life that she and Daddy were going to take her home to live with them. When I started crying because I didn't believe them and thought they were taking her to that awful prison instead, they promised me they weren't and they would be good to her. They said they could not take me because I was too little and too much trouble, but when I got older, they would. After they left I was so happy for my sister that I gave the doll to a little girl whose mother had just been killed in an accident. It made her feel a little better and we became friends.

By this time Annette had already left for a foster home, which just left me at the Children's Receiving Center.

I felt very proud because I had made all A's and had gotten good behavior awards for everything they had at the center. I just knew I was big enough to go home now, too.

However, I was soon to learn my good behavior and honest efforts were never going to be rewarded by going home. After I heard this, I was so upset I threw my supper on the floor and got the only spanking I ever had there. After the lady spanked me, she told me not to cry over people who didn't appreciate my efforts because she heard I was going to get a foster home the next week myself.

She was right about the foster home. However, I ended up in the hospital for an emergency tonsillectomy and missed the home completely. I was pretty happy because I got out of the hospital on my birthday and got to eat all the ice cream I wanted when I got back.

That was my seventh birthday. That year I was old enough to go to an amusement park on Orphan's Day. I was so happy that day to see Annette again. I spent the whole day with her and met my three big brothers I didn't even know I had.

By the time school started again I had given up the idea of ever getting a home. However, about a month after school started I went to a foster home with a family by the name of Bascum.

All I remember of the location was that it was in a very nice neighborhood and school. The home, however, was a disaster.

The woman promised me everything and gave me nothing. I was the only child there and always alone because the mother was always at some club and just left me notes every day what to do. I never got a hot meal because at seven I couldn't cook. My legs started swelling and hurt every night. I had a problem of wetting the bed after the tonsillectomy that I had had the summer before. She started pinning diapers on me at night and whipping me for wetting the bed, and when I showed her that my legs were swollen and hurting she just said it was because I was a bad girl and wet the bed.

She also made me wash the sheets by hand and stuck me with the pins so I would be good and not wet the bed. When I went to school one day they insisted I eat a hot lunch because I was so skinny. They had never seen me eat at school and were concerned about it.

When I told the mother that night, she was furious because she never allowed me to eat at school or pack a lunch. She made me strip off my clothes, and after she whipped me, she made me stand in the kitchen by myself without my clothes until she went to a club party and then got back home. I didn't even know how to tell time yet, but it seemed like she was gone forever. When she got home she pinned a diaper on me and made me walk around the block with a sign she made saying I wet the bed. I don't think I ever felt so terrible as when everyone on the block started laughing at me.

Someone didn't think it was funny because the next day a welfare worker came to the house. I was home because I refused to ever go back to school after that episode. She told the worker I was home sick, though, and I didn't argue the point when they told me to go outside and play so they could talk.

I don't know what was said, but that weekend I met the father of this home for the first time. He was a traveling sales-man and had never seen me until then. I really liked him. He played games and watched TV with me and even carried me upstairs and tucked me in bed that night. When I said I didn't want to wear diapers any more, he was upset about what his wife was doing. He didn't know anything that had happened. When he asked her what was going on in his home, she said I was a behavior problem and she was going to send me back to the orphanage. When he left again, I went back to the center feeling responsible for everything.

Childhood

I don't remember how long I was at the center this time, but it wasn't longer than a few weeks when I went to City Hospital for my first eye operation, as I was severely cross-eyed. This had not done much for my self-image. No one came to visit me, but I was a pretty jolly kid in spite of everything. I sang a lot while I was there. I was very disappointed when the operation was over and I was still as cross-eyed and ugly as ever.

I then went to a foster home outside Needham, Ohio. The people's name was Roberts. They lived in a nice house on a farm. I really liked this home very much, and the people were very young and nice to me. They let me feed the animals every day and even taught me to drive the tractor to the pasture at night to bring in the cows. I had my own room and a pet calf. They liked me very much, and I really loved them. I felt really happy and wanted for the first time in years. However, I was soon to be hurt again. The welfare never told me, but these people wanted to adopt me because they talked to me about being their very own little girl, and I said it would make me very happy. That's when my dad and stepmother showed up for the second time in my life. Three weeks later the family said the authorities felt I should be in a home where I would have other kids to play with. So I lost them forever.

I think the welfare was serious about other children, because the next home was in Needham, Ohio, city limits with 16 children from ages 9 weeks to about 19 years old. The parents' name was Mr. and Mrs. Fisher. I sure didn't have my own room or my own anything in that house. Things were so hectic that on my eighth birthday they even put the wrong name on the cake! I always thought if I ever got lost that nobody would ever miss me anyway. I started the third grade at Needham Elementary School. Believe it or not, even with all the changes in my life, I still maintained a straight-A average all through school.

It was in this home that the sexual abuse began with the older boys living in the home. I was not their only victim though. There were two other little girls, just about 10 and 11 years old. I soon began hating these boys as well as myself because I didn't know how to stop what was going on and was too frightened to tell any adults.

I was almost happy when a welfare worker came to take me to City Hospital for eye surgery again. I knew I could sleep at night for a week anyway. As it happened, though, the foster mother felt because of the surgery and my very small size for my age that with so many others at home to take care of, I should be moved. Although I liked her I was very much relieved because of the situation with these boys.

When I woke up from the operation there were bandages all around my head and eyes and I was sick with pneumonia from the ether they had given me for the operation.

This time I had a visitor. A very nice lady was giving me crushed ice and saying I would be OK. At first I thought it was a nurse. She then told me she was going to be my new mommy and that my new daddy was there, too, helping her take care of me. They took turns staying day and night at the hospital until I was well enough to go home with them. These were the people that to this very day I consider the only real mother and dad I ever had.

They lived on Arnold Avenue in the West End. Their names were Mr. and Mrs. Kirk. Although the operation had done nothing to help my eyes or their looks, I did not feel ugly this time because Mrs. Kirk got my hair cut and a permanent. She made me pretty dresses and even bought little bows to match for my hair. I felt like I was very pretty, as she always told me that beauty is only skin deep and what is in your heart is what really shows your true beauty. Every night we all three took a walk and every Sunday we went to church. I learned all about God and wanted to get baptized. When they asked the welfare, they told them my real dad said no. The Kirks and I were upset about this and talked to the minister together. He felt my father did not have that right under the circumstances. The minister signed the consent himself. I was so happy and proud. There wasn't much anyone could do after I had been baptized to prevent it.

We then moved to Pendergrass Avenue in the West End. I went to school at Washington Elementary School on Elm Street. I was happy and loved.

I had a third eye operation while I was there. The operation results were still the same. I went back to school as soon as I could and continued my good grades. I really liked my fourth grade teacher, too. Mr. and Mrs. Kirk went to open house and joined the P.T.A. at school. Mr. Kirk became ill with hay fever and was told he should move to a better climate. They had recently adopted a baby girl that I loved very much. They then applied to adopt me, too. The welfare immediately contacted my father, who flat out refused. We were all brokenhearted, and I vowed I would never let myself love anyone else again. The Kirks felt that since my father wanted to control my life, he and my stepmother should be made to keep me themselves. Since Mr. and Mrs. Kirk had six months before they moved, the welfare set up weekend visits with my dad and stepmother. I did not like the idea at all. However, the Kirks did not want me to continue being tossed around if there was any chance my real family could keep me.

The weekends were miserable. When my stepmother wasn't working, she was drinking. I met my stepsister for the first time. She was the same age as Julia. Julia hated me and unfortunately she got to take care of me when I was home on weekends. She would beat on me, pull my hair, throw water in my face. When she held me out the fourth-floor window by my feet to drop me, a neighbor caught her in time. I did not have to go for any more weekends and never saw Julia again until welfare handed her my own two children three years ago.

When the Kirks had to leave, we were all simply torn apart. I went to a religious home in Smithfield, Ohio. It was in a beautiful area. It was an all-girls boarding school. The religion was a big change for me. This in itself was very confusing for me. I really did become very upset and troubled. I wanted my mommy and daddy Kirk. What really hurt was I knew they wanted me.

By then I was 10 years old. They had their own school on the grounds. I never had any visitors on visiting days, so I was allowed to stay at the main building and go get the other kids from their cottages for their visitors. I was still skinny and sick a lot. I didn't like it there at all. One time I spilled food on my uniform and had to stand and watch the other kids eat for two whole days without any food. Another time I couldn't eat a jelly sandwich because I was full and didn't like it. I got the same sandwich every meal for three days until I ate it. The one school supervisor would have an older girl bring me in to her every night for a whipping. I would go back to the cottage every night and cry most of the night. I really began then to act out.

I felt nobody in the whole world cared any more and neither did I. I would hide in the weeds so I would miss church. When a cook offered me a dime to lock the bathroom door on one of the teachers, I took her up on the offer. Before I started getting in trouble, my dad and stepmother started showing up every visiting day and making promises every week that they didn't keep. I think it was the disappointments every week that started most of this behavior.

I was having a lot of physical problems during this time. I had a cold continuously and swelling in my legs and arms. The home began taking me to City Hospital Clinic every week for different tests, vitamins, and some kind of physical therapy. I also spent most of the time in the infirmary at the home in bed.

A couple of weeks later I went to court. At the time I didn't know where I was. My real dad was there and Julia and my real mother, but I did not get to see her. I sat on a bench in the hall while everyone went in the courtroom. I still did not know I was at the courthouse. I was 11 years old at this time.

I was sitting on a bench in the hallway of the courthouse when two young men in nice suits came up and started talking to me. They asked me if I ever saw a pink elephant. I thought they were nuts, so I said no, the only one I ever saw was checkered.

I found out years later that they were doctors who were supposed to be testing me at my probate hearing. I didn't even know I was in a courthouse, much less sitting outside my own trial.

Ordeal at
Chatwood

2

The next day, a welfare worker came to the orphanage and said she was taking me to a new and beautiful home with plenty of kids and a nice school and all new clothes. I was a little confused and happy that at last I was going to get adopted by a nice family.

Something was certainly wrong with this worker's story. She had to be the world's greatest liar because she took me instead straight to Chatwood Psychiatric Hospital where I was locked up with a bunch of screaming old ladies that scared me to death. They put me in a bathtub and scrubbed me from head to foot with some smelly soap. Then they told me I was here to stay and I had to take four shots [probably Thorazine] a day. Then I said I wasn't going to stay or take any shots because I wasn't sick. They threw me on the floor and gave me a shot right then. I still knew I was right, but after that I sure didn't argue with them about anything. I just took whatever came my way.

After several months on the receiving ward at Chatwood I was finally transferred to the Children's Unit. My dad and step-mother came one Sunday and we were sitting in a yard swing close to the main gate. My dad said he worked there for a while and helped build all the tunnels and he could tell me how to get out. By then I had just turned 12. I told him I wasn't a fool: if I wanted out bad enough all I had to do was walk out the front gate and get on a bus. I also asked him if he wanted me to get out so bad, why did he put me in there in the first place? He said I was sick a lot and needed operations for my eyes and he couldn't pay for it. At that time, he sounded sensible so I believed him and even felt sorry for him. However, when I told Miss Ely, who was a social worker there, she was very angry about what he said, because it was not the truth. She said I did not even belong there at all, but it was too late to cry over spilled milk. I really marvel at how something this terrible can happen to anyone and just be written off by very professional people with something as simple as an old-time phrase.

I felt really bad when I heard Annette was coming to see me the next day and Miss Ely had left orders that none of my family could ever visit again. I had not seen her in a couple of years. When they stopped her at the door, I started crying and tried to run to her. They put her and her foster mother out and put me in the quiet room for getting upset about it. I never had a chance to see her again until the trial with my own children three years ago.

After that, I only had visitors one time. They let my stepmother come one Sunday because she had a check for a song I had written while I was in the orphanage. When she came, I was very depressed because I was tied to the bed with plastic bags over both feet to keep me from handling them. They were in really bad condition, with my toes half rotting off and swollen to my ankles. I still don't know what was wrong with them, but after a couple months they finally got well.

When the nurse brought her in, she had Julia and my stepsister, Debra, with her. They were all dressed like a million dollars, my stepmother had diamonds all over. When they let my hands loose so I could sign the check, I was excited that my song was good enough to be published. However, when I started to see how much the check was for, my stepmother just turned it over and said to sign it. She said I was not allowed to see because I was "underage." I guess I will never know how much it was. The only thing I ever got was what she left that day to buy a pair of glasses for me.[1]

I really wish someday I could be rich enough to hire a private investigator. Not just for this incident, but because someone always had money in my account at the orphanage and all the time at Chatwood and everywhere I went afterwards. When I asked who was sending it, they said it was no one in my family and I was not to ever be told who.

After my 14th birthday, I was told that I had a foster home. On the following Saturday a real old man with crippled hands came to pick me up for the weekend. When I asked him if he was going to be my new grandpa, he laughed and said he would be my dad. I couldn't believe it.

These people's name was Mr. and Mrs. Engle. They lived on a farm near Marshfield, Ohio. They were very nice to me, but were very old. After three weekend visits, they decided they couldn't keep me.

Several months after this disappointment, I went to a horse farm outside Marshfield, Ohio. These people's name was Simons. They were a younger couple with five children. I admit everything that met the eye looked good. However, it was terrible. They wanted me to do all the work and take care of the younger kids. The couple was separated when they got me, and I think the lady saw an easy income with a free maid and babysitter combined. When I threatened to run away after several months, because the lady was gone for weeks at a time and I had to do everything including take care of her children, she sent me back to Chatwood. She told them I was selfish and very ungrateful for everything she had done for me and that I needed more discipline than she could give me.

I finally went to a home in Centerville later that year. I was almost 14 years old. I started the ninth grade at Centerville High School. This was very hard as they did not have any school at Chatwood. So I went from the fifth grade to the ninth with what I could only teach myself the years between that. In spite of this, my grades were fair.

The people's name was Mr. and and Mrs. Garrett. They had a nine-year-old son, Lewis. I liked Lewis, but I hated the parents. Mrs. Garrett worked with retarded children somewhere and told me all the time that I was just a vegetable and that vegetables don't have any feelings and whatever she did or said to me that I better keep my mouth shut and be thankful that anyone would ever keep me. She was always pulling my hair, throwing me on the floor, and beating on me constantly. She made me wear my dresses real big and down to my ankles so the kids would laugh at me and be able to see what a vegetable looked like. When somebody would come to visit, she would lock me in my room and tell them how retarded I was.

When I started growing personal hair, she would come in the bathroom when I was taking my bath and make me shave my privates. She told me I had to because I wasn't normal and my body was growing faster than my mind ever would. She said the men would want to take advantage of me. She didn't know it, but her husband was the only one who tried to take advantage of me. I hated her and was scared to death of her. She went out a lot at night. Her husband had the key to my bedroom door. She would lock me in, but after she would leave, he would come in and bother me. I was afraid to tell her, so I called my stepmother one time and told her. She just laughed at me and said I was going to be a tramp just like my real mother was. I never knew my real mother, but I hadn't ever heard anything good about her. This really upset me because I didn't want to be like her.

We had a lady gym teacher at school. I really liked her, but she was big and acted rough. One day I was talking in class and she took me in her office to swat me. It scared me so much I passed out. When she brought me to, she still gave me a good whipping, but then she said she had been wanting to talk to me anyway. She said she noticed I had been shaved when we took our showers for gym class, and wanted to know why. I wouldn't answer her because I was scared and really didn't know how to answer that without getting in real trouble when I went home. The gym teacher then said if I didn't answer her she was going to get a hold of me again. At that point I wasn't sure who scared me the most.

I started crying and told her the truth about Mrs. Garrett. I was still afraid to say anything about her husband. I was surprised when the teacher picked me up and held me in her arms and let me cry. She was crying, too. She convinced me she wouldn't tell them what I said to her. She also wanted to know why they never sent a worker to check on me. I wondered why myself but thought it was because I was from Chatwood. She made me feel good because she said I wasn't a vegetable and that I was pretty and intelligent. I was prettier now because I had a fourth eye operation in Chatwood, which had straightened out my eyes. I started seeing the gym teacher every week as she was also a school counselor.

I'm sure she reported the home situation to someone, because six weeks later, when school was out, I was moved again. This time I went to a home between Clemens and Marshfield, Ohio. It was in the country.

The name of these people was Mr. and Mrs. South. They had three children, a daughter, Lisa Mae, who was three months younger than me, a son, Wendell, who was almost 14, and a son, Bill, about 6 years old.

The mother and father in this home fought and argued continuously over nothing. The two older children were from a former marriage of Mrs. South. The youngest son was from their marriage. I did not like her daughter at all. She was always putting her hair in fancy styles and thought she was better than anyone else. Although I had just turned 15 a week after I went there, and Lisa Mae would be 15 in three months, she had been dating boys since she was 11 years old.

She had a steady boyfriend and told her mother she would not do any work at home because she was not going to be a slave for anyone. She felt that when she got a husband, then she would work in the house.

I felt sorry for Mrs. South because she always said she was sick. She had had a hysterectomy after her six-year-old was born. She also had a thyroid problem of some kind. I gladly did all the work there was to do and even let her teach me how to cook. I would have gladly done anything to keep from going back to Chatwood and felt that someday, when I was grown, it would help me to be a good wife and a good mother. Doing the work also helped my nerves when they were arguing.

I started the 10th grade at Marshfield High School. I was a little disappointed when they did not accept two of my credits from Centerville High and I had to carry extra subjects that year. With all the work I had to do at home, along with the extra subjects in school, it put a lot of strain on me.

As if this, added to the constant arguing, were not enough to deal with, her son, Wendell, was bugging me constantly to give in to him. I tried to explain to him what I had already been through and that I wanted him to just be a brother to me. This did not influence him whatsoever. He even started sneaking in my room at night.

His mom slept on the couch all the time next to the room I was in. I guess the sleeping pills kept her out. I was determined that this was not going to happen to me again because I still had nightmares from previous experiences. I decided before I let him touch me I would scream for her. When I started hollering for her, she came in all right.

Wendell was a good liar. He said I had a nightmare and he came in to see if I was all right. When I tried to tell her what happened, she grabbed a belt and started beating me and yelling at me not to call her son a liar. I certainly never tried to get help from her again. When I could at all possibly avoid Wendell completely, I did, and when I couldn't, I hated myself.

I kept hoping that I would meet a boy I liked in school and be able to date and get married to someone who would be good to me and love me. Although Wendell continued bothering me every chance he got, I met just the boy at school I had been hoping for all along.

Howard O'Dell and I were in the same grade in school. We were both 10th graders. Mrs. South would not let me go out on a date because she needed me at home, but she let Howard come to our house after school. He would pick flowers on his way up every night for me and even helped me with the work.

He gave me his class ring the next year in school. We still weren't allowed to date, but he still wanted to go with me. He never tried to bother me and when I told him about Wendell and that I hated him, he even beat Wendell up and told him to leave me alone.

That year Mrs. South did let me go to the prom with him if his mom and dad would take us. They really liked me and we had a nice time.

Howard and I were both 16 then. We really cared for each other. Our senior year we decided to date others to be sure we were going to want each other for life. I dated a few other boys that year, but my heart was still with Howard. By the time the prom came that year, we knew we wanted each other and decided on a July wedding.

I didn't know I had to get an OK from Chatwood as well as the Souths. I was upset because I had never told Howard anything about being from Chatwood. When I told him, he said it didn't make any difference, that he still loved me and would even go with me to ask them and let them meet him. I was so happy.

We were partners in our graduation class. We had both won an art scholarship that year and were going to go to the same college after we got married. When we graduated on May 29th, 1961, we made arrangements for a meeting at Chatwood with a doctor to ask about the wedding. At this time he was 18 and I was still seventeen until June 15th.

We never got to keep that appointment or the wedding because a week later Howard went to the college to see where we would be going. On his way home he was killed in an accident with an oil truck. The accident was so bad they didn't open the casket. It was just as well for me because I could not make myself go to his funeral. I wanted to remember him as the living, smiling boy I loved.

Since I had no one to talk to about how I felt, I silently cried and ached inside. Soon I got a job at a restaurant and it helped my grief somewhat.

Note

1. Rose's poem was based on a dream she had when she was 10 years old. The next morning, she shared the poem with a teacher, who smoothed out the words and phrasing a bit. Another teacher put it to music. The quarterly records at the orphanage do not mention the poem. However, the cadence of the lines is similar to Rose's later poems. A few phrases, such as "moving hand" and "endless space," may have been a teacher's idea. A search of religious songs has failed to locate it in any published song book.

In any event, the poem shows that Rose felt close enough to some of the teachers at the orphanage to share her dream and poem. The religious nature of the poem indicates that the religious instruction that she was receiving served to sustain her morale.

I Make the Sign of the Cross

I make the sign of the cross tonight
And speak my Savior's name.
Although today not all was right,
He will love me just the same.

He will listen to my feeble song,
And blend it into his choir.
He will take me to his breast so strong,
With arms that never tire.

There is no book, or strand of Holy beads,
To count each child in his care.
He knows and loves his own everywhere.

There is no dark or empty place,
But filled by him with light.
His moving hand through endless space,
Keeps all his world aright.

Approaching
Independence

3

By this time, Wendell was almost 18 and had a 20-year-old girl pregnant. I must say this did not surprise me like it did his mother. The girl, Jane, already had a four-month-old baby and wasn't married. Mrs. South was crying and asking me what she should do about it. I told her I didn't know, but marriage didn't sound like a bad idea under their circumstances. She said if they got married they would have to live with us and I would have to take care of the baby Jane had already. When they moved in, I took little Danny right away. I learned soon why Mrs. South wanted me to take care of Danny. Jane did not want him or Wendell's baby, which she was carrying. I loved Danny and took him everywhere I went. When he could talk, he started calling me Mommy.

The next summer I was 19. I couldn't stand all the pressure of working at the restaurant, taking care of all the work at home, and the full responsibility of little Danny, too. He was almost two. I loved him, as well as little Wendell, but he was not my baby or my responsibility. I was still broken up over Howard's death, even though it had been a year.

I ran away and stayed with a neighbor up the road. A few days later when we were talking I mentioned Mrs. Cooper, who was the first foster mother I could remember. When I mentioned her name, my neighbor said she knew an old couple that lived in Waterford by that name.

Since Waterford was less than three miles away, we decided to go and find out. Her sister knew them well and lived next door to them. As it turned out, they were the same people. They remembered me and were happy to see me again. The old man had lost his leg and couldn't walk. He would go to the car on crutches and drive, though.

They wanted me to come back and live with them, so my neighbor and her sister took me and Mrs. Cooper to Chatwood to ask. I was scared they were going to lock me up when I got there because I had run away from Mrs. South. They said they did have the police looking for me, but since I had a place to stay now, they wouldn't keep me. When we went back to Mrs. South's to get my things, she was waiting for me with a belt.

Since my neighbor and her sister went in with me she didn't hit me. When little Danny ran to me, Wendell grabbed him and held him back. He said he didn't want a scag touching his baby. This really tore me apart, since I had raised him for almost two years. It really hurt Danny because he never spoke a word from that day until he was nearly 10 years old. Before I left that day, he could talk good for his age. He called me Mommy, he knew the commercials on T.V. and most of my records by heart since I played them and sang to him all the time. I guess I shouldn't feel guilty because he never talked after that, but I still feel like it was my fault because he loved me so much.

After I went to live with the Coopers again, it was not the same. They were old and grumpy. Mrs. Cooper called Chatwood every day until she got her first check for me. I got a job at the grocery store in Waterford and gave her money besides the check she got from the state for keeping me. She was happy then, but still they were both well into their seventies.

I told her I wanted to get my own apartment in town. I got an apartment in the Waterford Hotel right next door to my job. I was so happy and proud to be on my own. Since I was still under age by two years, I didn't want the hospital to find out I had left the Coopers. I don't know if they found out. I loved my job and my home. I even began to date my boss's nephew, who was 21.

The next summer I was on the softball team and broke my hand while playing. This was really awful for me because I couldn't run the cash register or dip ice cream, so I lost my job. I was heartsick because I had to give up my home, too.

The same neighbor who helped me before said she had a sister in Central City who was separated from her husband and had two boys, six and ten years old. She said Greta wanted me to live with her and take care of the house and the boys while she worked. It sounded like a good idea for everyone.

I liked Greta very much. I also liked the boys. They treated me just like their big sister. Greta took us to the show on Sunday and came back to get us. She paid me $10 a week besides.

She had a boyfriend and was gone quite a bit. She talked to me about Elton (her former husband and the boys' father) quite a bit, but I had never met him myself until about three months later, when he came to see the boys. I told him Greta wasn't home, but he came in to see them anyway.

When she got home, her boyfriend was with her. She got so mad because Elton was there that she threw me out right then. It was snowing and I didn't have anywhere to go. When Elton offered me a ride to my dad and stepmother's house, if they would take me, I said I would appreciate that. I walked to the gas station and looked the number up. My stepmother said I could stay there a couple of weeks until I found a place to go.

After Elton took me there, he started coming regularly and wanted to take me out. He was a lot older than me, almost 20 years. My stepmother really liked him and kept insisting that I should marry him. I wasn't as interested in him as she was, but when he showed up with an engagement ring, she said to marry him or leave. That was what I did. I didn't love him, but I was faithful to him and tried my best to make it work out.

I have to admit, my wedding day was very disappointing right from the beginning. My stepmother wanted me to wear the dress I still had from the prom. She and my dad put together the cheapest wedding they could in their own living room. There was only her and Dad, Elton and I, one friend and her husband from the country, and the preacher.

I never wanted to back out of anything in my life so bad, but I wasn't sure what might happen if I tried. Although I had never mentioned anything to them about Howard, I was certainly having a lot of mixed feelings.

Marriage

4

Right after our wedding, we went to the apartment Elton already had. I didn't know at the time that his mother was living there, too. When I met her I was a little curious why she wasn't at her son's wedding. When I asked her she got down the Bible and began telling me what a sinner I was. She said I was committing adultery since Elton's ex-wife was still living. By now I was totally confused and miserable.

We were married on January 14, 1964. Since I had not been with Elton before we were married, he was angry to find out I had been with someone before him. I guess I was dumb, but it just never occurred to me to tell him. Just when I started to tell him about my life and the sexual abuses, he jumped up and went to bed on the couch. Then he said to make a list of everyone I had been with. I felt then that I didn't really owe him any explanation.

Since I was feeling angry myself, I got a piece of paper and wrote down every boy's name I had ever heard mentioned in my life. After I handed him the paper, he never mentioned anything to me about it again.

This is just one example of his many strange behaviors. For example, we'd be sitting at the table eating and talking about something good when suddenly he would jump up and start wrecking the kitchen. When I would get hold of him and try to talk to him, he would say he thought of something Greta had said or done to hurt him years ago.

Living with Elton was never having anything in the house to eat, not being allowed to talk to anyone much, or have any friends. I think that's why I looked forward to his boys coming to stay on the weekends. They were not strangers to me and I liked them very much.

After Elton and I married, however, the boys started to treat me differently. David, the oldest, hardly talked to me at all, and Elton was always mean to him. Timmy would run through the house tearing down curtains and undoing everything I would try to fix or clean up. He would kick and cuss me constantly. Although it wasn't easy, I tried to understand how he felt and loved him. Elton would not try to help with him at all because he thought he was cute and would laugh about everything he did.

I was concerned about both the boys, so I decided to talk to Greta. She was nicer than I expected her to be. She told me that Elton had spent nine months on a mental ward while he was in the Marines and that he was subject to these sudden mood changes because of a split personality. She said that because of the bad life I had had, I would be wise to leave him. We also decided the boys would do better if they didn't come over for a while.

We had been married almost two years now, and Elton was treating me worse. We had moved upstairs in the building where my dad and stepmother were living. The only time Elton really acted normal was around them. One day my stepmother came up to see me when I was alone. She said she was mad enough to kill me. When I asked her why, she said Elton had come down before he went to work and said I had woke him up during the night and accused him of being with her. I told her I didn't know what he was talking about, and I might have been dreaming and said something to him.

She said that was possible and asked me how he was treating me as a wife. I didn't believe she really wanted to know out of concern for me, but I was desperate to talk to someone. I told her that in the two years we had been married that he had only made love to me about a dozen times and then only because I had cried and begged him to show he cared. She said he would talk to her a lot and cry about missing his boys, and maybe I should think about having a baby. Somehow I never felt that having a baby was a solution for saving anyone's marriage, but I had wanted a baby for quite some time. I decided to talk to Elton about my feelings. I was really surprised when for the first time since we were married he held me in his arms and started crying. It really made me feel happy and needed to think of being a mother.

Marriage

The worst part was when I couldn't get pregnant. So when Elton would get angry and say it had to be me, I couldn't argue that point since he was already a father. I was beginning to feel like I couldn't do anything right. Finally, I gave up and went to a doctor. The doctor told me I had only one chance for having a baby of my own. He said the reason I wasn't able to get pregnant was because my womb was lying flat against my spine and would take a lot of turning to get it into the right position and even then I might not be able to carry a baby to term. He then suggested that I consider adoption. I didn't fully understand all of this, but I certainly had a lot to think about on my way home.

After Elton and I talked it over, we decided to contact an adoption agency. About a week later a very nice lady came to see us and fill out papers. She said she thought we had a good chance and we would hear from her in a couple of weeks. I had started working at a dime store near our apartment. I was really nervous and excited while waiting for an answer, so working really helped.

I happened to be off work the day she called. We were turned down because of our age difference and the fact that Elton was already divorced and had a family. I was really disappointed and very sad.

I then decided to take the treatments and try to have my own child. This was in October of 1965. By February of 1966, I was pregnant. I was very happy, but also concerned about being able to carry it. I had a lot of faith in my doctor and God, though. When Elton found out I was pregnant at last, instead of being happy he changed his mind completely and said he never wanted me to have a damn brat for him to have to support when he already had two. I was so upset and depressed with his sudden change in attitude that I tried to kill myself.

Although I had thought of this before in my life, this was the first time I really tried. The only thing that saved me was when he broke down the bathroom door and took the razor away from me.

He said he didn't care about me, but I should think about my baby and that it would die, too. Most of what Elton said to me didn't mean anything, but I thank God he chose the right words for once.

I decided then to forget Elton and live for my baby I had wanted so much. I knew that after the baby was born I would have to leave Elton for both our sakes. Somehow, for the rest of my pregnancy, the depression never lifted. I slept continuously, and there was never much to eat. As the baby grew, it put a lot of pressure on my spine, making it hard for me to walk. The doctor told me to stay off my feet as much as possible the last two months because the longer I could carry it, the better chance the baby would have.

On December 14, 1966, I had a very beautiful baby boy. When the nurse brought him in and put him in my arms, I felt as beautiful and happy as the Mother Mary must have felt herself. There was Christmas music playing in the hospital and a new snow falling outside. I named the baby Kirk.

Elton was not there when Kirk was born. When they told me I had a visitor, I knew it was Elton and when he saw Kirk he would have to be happy, too.

I was really surprised when instead my dad and stepmother came in. When I asked them if they had seen Elton, my stepmother said he had had supper with them, but he wasn't coming to the hospital to see me so he asked them to come for him. I was glad when they left.

I had some complications during delivery and wasn't feeling real strong yet. That night I had a 105-degree fever and was put in isolation because of all the babies. The doctor and nurses worked with me all night and the next day trying to break the fever. They tried to get ahold of Elton and couldn't. My fever finally broke later that afternoon.

Since I was so sick, I wasn't allowed to go home, so they finally called Elton and got him. They asked him to take Kirk home anyway. He flat out refused, so they had to keep us both or call the welfare to come and get Kirk until I got well.

Finally, after two weeks, Kirk and I could both go home. They had kept Kirk in the nursery the whole time and had him spoiled rotten.

I found out Elton had been staying with Greta and the kids while I was gone. I stayed with Elton until he ordered me to leave when Kirk was 10 months old. I was ready to leave anyway, as Elton had started abusing Kirk. He wouldn't buy groceries or anything we needed. I had gone back to work by then and was preparing to leave.

The night he threw us out, it was November 25, 1967. It was freezing cold and we didn't have anywhere to go. I had $2, so I called a cab and went as far as I could go. I was working at a department store on Flemming Road. When the $2 ran out, I started walking. It was below zero, and I was afraid Kirk would freeze, so I took my coat off since I had a sweater on, too, and I wrapped Kirk in my coat. I don't know how far I walked before a car pulled up and offered us a ride.

Since it was almost 10 o'clock at night, it scared me. When I said no, the man said I was a crazy kid to be out then. I finally agreed to let him take us to the store where I worked.

I went to my boss, who was an older lady. She took Kirk and me home with her until I got an apartment. I rented an apartment next door to my baby-sitter. There wasn't any furniture or heat, so after three days I had to give it up.

I had no other choice but to call my stepmother to see if we could stay there until I found another apartment. I had paid a month's rent on the other one and couldn't get my money back. I told her it would only be three weeks. She said I could stay, but I would have to board Kirk at my sitter's house all the time. I agreed to do this and went to see Kirk after work every day.

Two weeks later, I got an apartment right next door. It was furnished. The apartment wasn't beautiful, but to me and Kirk it was heaven. We were finally settled together in our own home without any one to treat us mean. The lady downstairs took care of him while I worked. It felt so good to be able to feed him good food and all he wanted to eat. It also made me feel good to take him out when I got paid and buy him clothes or a little toy.

Divorced
and Lonely

5

My divorce was final in March 1968. I met a guy at work I really fell for. Gene was a nice guy but he decided to marry someone else. He never knew how much I really cared about him. During the time I was getting over Gene, his brother, Walter, caught me on the rebound.

Walter was different than Gene, as he had a drinking problem. It sounds terrible to say, but by this time I didn't care much about myself at all. I was so tired of feeling lonely and always being thrown out that it made me feel needed and not so lonely seeing Walter. I loved Kirk very much, but he couldn't fill all the loneliness I was feeling.

I was still working at the store when Kirk was 18 months old. I got pneumonia and had to quit for a while. The department at work took up a collection to pay the rent and food that week. There was also a labor dispute at that time so my job was terminated. I was hardly well in a week but I had to look for another job.

I started working at a restaurant up the street from 7 P.M. to 8 A.M. I just didn't make enough money at this job, so I began working days, too, at a dime store also close by. As you can imagine, it wasn't easy working two jobs and taking care of a one-and-a-half-year-old at the same time.

I didn't pay much attention to feeling tired and losing weight until I passed out at work. I went to City Hospital emergency the next day, since I didn't have insurance on either job. I got a nice lady doctor who ran some tests on me. When she

37

came back in, she said I had more problems than just working two jobs. She said I was also pregnant.

I don't think I ever felt so mixed up in my life. I sat there for an hour before I could say anything at all. I was feeling so many different emotions that I think I was honestly afraid to move or talk to anyone. I finally told her I didn't know how that was possible because I was taking birth control pills. She said that with all the working and different hours, I had probably missed some.

She got the usual family situation at home and suggested I think about adoption. That was where we parted. I went home after getting an appointment for the clinic. No matter what, I knew in my heart I would never give my baby away.

When I finally got Walter sober enough to tell him, he had a worse idea than the doctor. He said he would pay for an abortion. I threw him out and never saw him until about two years later.

I continued working days at the store but gave up the night job and started going to the Murray Hill Clinic in the neighborhood. I had to quit work when I was about four months pregnant because of the company policy. I was glad in a way, as I was having a lot of leg and back pain anyway. The only choice I had now was to turn to welfare until I could get back to work.

My stepmother and her daughter, Debra, told me if I went to the welfare that they would take the baby and Kirk away from me because I wasn't married, and that I had done Kirk a great wrong by getting pregnant and being a tramp. I was so scared I carried Kirk up and down the streets for three days trying to find a job. Nobody, however, would hire me in my condition and I had to give up. I prayed all day and night before I went to the welfare. I got a very nice worker about my age who thought my stepsister and mother were pretty weird and wondered why they didn't help me and Kirk. I told her a little bit about my family not raising me, and we did get on ADC temporarily.

The only drawback about getting on ADC was that I had to agree to file charges against Walter and prove he was the baby's father. I guess I sounded silly when I asked the worker how I was supposed to prove it. She said through blood tests and witnesses to the fact that I was only dating him. Since none of this could be done until after the baby was born, it gave me time to work on other things until then.

The apartment I had did not allow more than one child, so I had to find another apartment. We then moved to Woodburn

Avenue in Murray Hills. The apartment was bigger but was on the fourth floor, and with a two-year-old this was a big worry. I couldn't open the windows, and it got a little hard carrying Kirk up and down the stairs.

At this time, my stepsister really got involved in our lives. She would call three or four times a day and tell me if there was anything dirty or out of place in my house when she came over that I would lose Kirk and that she and my stepmother would help Elton get him away from me.

I was having a very difficult pregnancy anyway. My legs were swollen twice their normal size all the time, and I had trouble being able to sleep at night. I knew, too, with the $136 a month income and $26 in food stamps that it was impossible to eat right. Since I had made some friends in the building, most of whom were either working or disabled and couldn't always do their own laundry, it gave me an idea. Since I had my own wringer washer, I started doing their washing and ironing to make extra money. I knew none of them could pay very much, but I made every dollar count.

I did feel a little better with more to eat and the work to fill my free time. I even started buying a dozen diapers or a package of T-shirts or some little thing I knew the new baby would need, if I had a few dollars left over.

Kirk and I loved each other so much, and he was as excited about a new baby as I was. He would try to help with the laundry and dishes, and I would even let him pick out some of the things for the baby. I was so sure I was going to have a girl that I bought all girls' things.

My stepsister couldn't stand us being happy. One day Miss Moore, the worker I had, came out to see me. She said she had been getting phone calls every day from some lady about me having men coming and going all the time. What really made it look bad for me was that the only place I had to dry the washings was on lines in my kitchen. There were men's underwear and clothes hanging all over my kitchen.

I told her the truth about the laundry and showed her what I had bought the baby. She was really happy since she could only give me a $20 voucher for the baby after it was born. I also cried and told her that if I was doing wrong with all these imaginary men, how come I would sit at the foot of four flights of steps with a baby in one arm and groceries in the other and cry because I couldn't hardly make it up the stairs at eight months?

She told me to stop crying because she knew I was telling her the truth and she was proud of what I was trying to do for my children. She also said to be careful because someone did not feel the same way that she did.

All the time my stepsister was doing these things to me, she was telling me it had to be some of my neighbors because she loved me and only threatened me to try and straighten me out.

The way Debra and my stepmother were acting, I thought they were really decent. I was shocked when Debra said she had always hated her mother because she wasn't married when she had her and still can't forgive her because she didn't give her away. I told her that I already loved my baby and if I kept it the same as Kirk that I would always know where it was and how it was being treated, and that it wouldn't have to suffer like I had and grow up hating its mother. I also told her I could sleep at night knowing they were both in my love and care.

She then said that if I kept the baby that Kirk would always hate me because of what I did. I didn't believe I was doing wrong to keep my baby, or that I was doing Kirk wrong either. I felt the same responsibility to both of them.

Two weeks later my neighbors gave me a surprise baby shower because I had worked so hard to get things together. It really made me feel good.

I went into labor on May 21, 1969. I called the Murray Hill Clinic, and they sent me to City Hospital. When I got there, they asked me when the baby was due. I told them it had been due on the 20th. I was having contractions, but they said I wasn't ready to deliver and to go home and take the Darvon they gave me when I had pains.

I did what they said, but on the 23rd I was getting sharper and more frequent pains so I went back to the hospital. They kept me that night and even prepared me for delivery. I told them the clinic had said to tell them the baby was transverse, live, and they would know what I meant. They then said they would take an X-ray in the morning.

However, the next morning I had a different doctor and instead he said even though I was contracting that I still wasn't ready. He sent me back home to take the Darvon.

My stepsister came down that night with her husband and said if I didn't help myself to have the baby that it might die. There was a neighbor who said she had been a nurse, and she and Debra had me pulling on the refrigerator and on ropes they had tied to the bed. I didn't understand anything they were doing, but I didn't want to lose the baby. They were even prepared to deliver it.

I was really in pain and frightened. Somehow I knew if I didn't get the right kind of help, the baby wasn't the only one who would be lost. I was swollen all over and even my face was swollen and puffy. Debra's husband did not hold still for what they were doing and called the life squad.

When they arrived and checked me out, they said I couldn't have the baby on my own because it was too large, and we wouldn't either one make it. This was at 3 A.M. on May 25th. They rushed me back to City Hospital. They took me back to the second floor again. They told me they didn't have any records yet from Murray Hill Clinic, and asked about the family medical history. I told them I really didn't know about my family that much.

They then gave me an IV to induce labor again and a stress test. Before the tests came back, another doctor came in to check me. He said I still wasn't dilating yet, when just then my water broke and the baby tried to come instantly.

Even though the baby was tearing me apart, I still couldn't have her. They rushed me into a room and forced the baby back enough to cross my legs and sit me up for a spinal block. As anyone can well guess, I was screaming with pain, as I hadn't even had an aspirin until the spinal. They held me for a few minutes in that position. Just as I started getting a little numb, I got a sharp pain that seemed to go straight to my head and I just fell silent.

They strapped me on a table and started cutting me. The next few minutes were even worse than all the pains. Then I could tell they had finally delivered the baby and everything got really quiet. Finally the doctor ordered a respirator for the baby and the worst time in my life was waiting to hear that baby cry. I know it was only a few seconds, but it seemed like hours until I finally heard her cry. She was so beautiful when the nurse brought her over to show me. Even with all the mess, she looked beautiful to me after all that.

In the recovery room I still had the pain in my head but I thought it was just because of all I had experienced and it would go away after I got some rest. The next day after she was born, I had a problem. When I started to raise up, I was numb all over and couldn't move anything. I couldn't say anything plain enough to understand.

There was a nurse in the room with someone else who noticed something was wrong and called for a doctor. Two doctors came running in and pulled me up under the arms and neck. When they did this the feeling started coming back. They asked me if I had had a spinal and then gave me a shot. After that I seemed to be OK.

I named my little girl Kathy Marie after my boss at the department store. Kathy was born May 26, 1969, on a Monday.

Kathy Is Born,
A Family of Three

6

I was anxious to see little Kirk's face when he saw me and his baby sister. He was two and a half now.

The day I was to go home, all I could see was all those steps I had to climb. I was still feeling as if I had been beaten. The doctor said to go up the steps backwards a few steps at a time. I had quite a few stitches and it would be easier on me.

When little Kathy and I got home, Kirk was so excited that he talked and ran around the house about four hours before he finally wound down. That same day the landlord and his secretary came to see the baby. They had gotten her a whole new outfit apiece and a set of pajamas. Their kindness, along with my neighbor's surprise shower earlier, made me feel really good. It also, for the first time in my life, helped me realize that there are good people in the world that do let someone know they care and that their efforts are noticed and appreciated.

The next morning Miss Moore sent a homemaker to help us out for a week. She was a grandmother herself and a real delight to have around. Her last day with us, we both noticed that Kathy had not cried at all and didn't look well either. Kathy was exactly 10 days old. When I took her temperature, it was 105 degrees. I called the Murray Hill Clinic. They said she was too young for the ordinary childhood diseases and to take her straight to City Hospital emergency.

The homemaker drove us out and I took Kirk with me. After hours of waiting, they finally called for Kathy. When they saw her, they told me to leave the room while they checked her. After about two more hours, they told me they needed a complete family medical history on me and the baby's father's family. I got on the phone and called my dad's house. My stepmother, as usual, was not volunteering anything except that I was the only one who ever had any kind of problems, and my problem was simply that I was crazy.

By this time I felt like I might be soon if I didn't get some answers from Kathy's dad's family. When I started to call Walter's mother, I realized she didn't even know I was pregnant or had the baby. When she got over the shock, she did tell me what she could about her family history. Regardless of what she said about me then, I was thankful for the information. I went and told the doctor what I could about her father's side.

Since I knew my baby wasn't crazy, I told the doctor the truth, that my family hadn't raised me and that I knew very little about them. He said that the only real choice I had left was to sign for a spinal tap on the baby. When I asked him why, he said he had a feeling she might have spinal meningitis. I don't know how I looked when he said this but I will never forget how I felt. I was so scared and confused that my head was spinning inside. I desperately needed someone to talk to that would just let me cry and hold me while I said all the things I was feeling.

At the same time, I was feeling very angry at my family and couldn't understand why they always rejected me and now my children. I prayed to God while I was signing the paper to help me do the right thing.

During this whole ordeal little Kirk was clinging to me and crying that he was hungry and his baby sister was going to die. Although I hadn't said anything, I was certainly afraid that she might. I knew Kirk was hungry, but all I had was money for bus fare home. I kept loving him and told him that the doctors and God would help little Kathy get well, but she had to stay at the hospital so they could help her.

Kirk was an exceptionally bright two-year-old. When the doctors said I could carry her upstairs myself after she was admitted, Kirk suddenly said, "Doctor, it's my baby, too, you know." The comment was so sudden and serious sounding that we all stood still for a minute. At this, the doctor took his hand and let him go up with us to see where she would be staying.

Since I didn't have anyone to keep Kirk at home, the doctor arranged for him to come to the hospital with me and see Kathy every day. Every day I fixed a lunch and we spent the day with Kathy. It was an awful feeling to see her lying there so helpless with all kinds of funny-looking attachments on her.

Even after I would go home at night I would call patient information to check on her. They never definitely told me what was wrong with her, and maybe they were never sure, but after two weeks she got well enough to go home.

Kathy's birth and the few long weeks afterward were beginning to really get the best of me physically as well as the emotional end of it. Although Kirk loved Kathy, he was a normal child who was beginning to feel left out and jealous of her. This worked out fine, though. Since she was OK, I could devote more time to him.

I was still having the headache from time to time, and my legs were still swollen and I felt like I wanted to cry most of the time. When Miss Moore came to see Kathy, she suggested I talk to a psychiatrist or someone who might be able to help me. No one who knew me knew that I had ever been in Chatwood, including her.[1] She had no way of knowing how the idea of going to a psychiatrist frightened me.

When I went back to the clinic for my six-week checkup, the doctor I had seen before was no longer there. I made another appointment for two weeks later. I decided to give Miss Moore's idea a try. I asked the clinic nurse if there were any psychiatrists in the city that didn't work at Chatwood. She gave me the strangest look and asked me what did I ask about Chatwood for? I told her I didn't know why, and she called me after I got home and told me to call Central Clinic at City Hospital. This was in August 1969 and they gave me an appointment for October.

My stepsister was still always threatening me and coming to see how clean the house was and the children. I have always been a good housekeeper, as all I ever did in most of the foster homes was clean house and take care of children. I was really getting fed up with this stepsister. When I would tell her I was, she would threaten me for getting smart with her and say I was just a little tramp.

When Kathy was exactly three months old, I was on the phone with my stepsister when the lady on the third floor came up to tell me she would watch the kids at her house while I went next door to get some groceries for us. This was the very first time I had left the kids with anyone since I quit work. When I hung up the phone, I took the kids down on my way out. Because of being on the fourth floor, it was impossible to carry the baby and hold onto Kirk and pull a grocery cart up the steps, too.

I was only gone 45 minutes. As I was coming back inside our building, two other ladies told me that the juvenile police were looking for me. I didn't think too much about it at first, since Elton's oldest boy, David, had been in a home for a while. I thought he had run away and maybe had tried to find me. When I got to my neighbor's on the third floor where the kids were and knocked on the door, a policewoman answered. My neighbor was standing behind her by another policewoman, crying. She had Kathy in her arms, but I didn't see Kirk. When I asked where he was, my neighbor said he was playing in the other room with her son.

Just then the officer at the door asked me my name. When I answered her, both officers grabbed me at the same time and literally threw me into a chair. I was too angry to be scared then. I started demanding to know what I had done wrong and started to get up. That was the wrong thing to do, as I didn't get far. They asked me if I had a lawyer, and I asked them what I needed one for.

At last they told me that some lady had called and told them I had left a two-year-old and a two-month-old baby alone on the fourth floor for two days. I found it hard to believe this whole thing was really happening. I told them exactly what really was going on and still had the grocery cart outside the door. Every time my neighbor tried to tell them the same thing I did, they told her to shut up. I asked who this lady was that called. When they said she didn't give her name, I wanted to know why they came to check on it anyway.

I wasn't being a smart aleck, because this was the first time I had even talked to a police officer. However, I really made the one angry because she grabbed me up out of the chair and asked me if I knew my rights. I didn't know what she meant by that and I said very loud that I had a right to be treated like a human being. She finally let go of me and said I was either totally innocent or the best con artist she ever met. I was happy when she said to take my kids and go on home. I did just that and until just this last year, other than their placements for the hospital stays I had or when I was working, I never left them with anyone again.

The next day, when I talked to my neighbor, it was obvious that she was as innocent and understandably as upset as I was. I think it is also plain to see why I was beginning not to trust anyone. I put a note on the door saying no more phone calls and absolutely no visitors. I began spending all my time with my kids or totally by myself if the kids were asleep. I couldn't sleep well at night and really began to hate myself more each day, because no matter how hard I tried to do what was right, whoever was making these phone calls to the different authorities was certainly making everything I did seem wrong.

Since none of these people could ever get a name for this lady, it made it next to impossible to confront her. For the next two weeks I couldn't seem to get my mind off of ending my life. I even began planning how. The only thing that stood in my way was those two beautiful children whom I knew loved me very much and didn't have anyone else in the world but me.

In a way this thought alone was frightening. I knew I had to hang on, but I wasn't sure how long I could. I don't really know why Miss Moore came out two days later for an unscheduled home visit. As usual, I didn't answer the door when I heard a knock. However, when she called my name and said who she was, I was afraid not to answer the door. When I let her in, she handed me the note I had put on the door and said it wasn't a very nice welcome for anyone who wanted to see me.

When she saw me, she said I looked terrible and should see a doctor. I told her it was still over two months until my appointment at Central Clinic. She told me I could go to the emergency room anytime and that I couldn't wait that long. She said I was a wonderful mother, but I would go crazy if I didn't start living for myself as well. After she left, I thought it over as well and decided to go.

Since the only real experiences I had had with a hospital other than the eye operations as a child and having my two babies were at Chatwood, I didn't know what to expect. I took the kids and went to City Hospital emergency room. After several hours, they called me in. I talked to a young lady as best I could about the constant fear of losing my children and crying most of the time. I was afraid to tell her about the plans or feelings I had of ending my life. When she gave me some tests with ink spots and different questions on a list she had, she told me that I wasn't mentally ill and to see a medical doctor, since my baby was so young I was probably still having some postnatal depression and it would pass.

I felt a little better when I left because what she had said made a lot of sense to me. I also felt it would be good for all of us to move away from there and try to make a new start. I finally found a second-floor apartment in a two-story house. In October 1969 we moved to Fourth Avenue in the West End. We all were happier and even had a yard. I didn't tell any of my neighbors where we were moving, just in case this lady did happen to be one of them. During this time, I avoided my stepsister whenever possible since she didn't do much to cheer me up. She did help me find the house I got, so she was the only one who knew where we lived. I still avoided her when I could.

Note

1. Rose's childhood psychiatric records were sealed.

The Battle for
Health and Children

7

The children and I started going to church on the bus in Mt. Filmore on Sundays. The only thing my new friends knew about me was that I was a divorcee with two children. We all made good friends at the church and were really happy for a change. Kirk was now three years old and Kathy was six months old. When I met Don Evans at church, we took to each other right away. He was the same age as me and studying to be a missionary. His mother was a very beautiful person, too.

Don Evans and I were very good friends. Besides his missionary studies, he also had a youth group that he managed. I helped with the group myself and it was good for me and the children since I could take them on the outings, too. When I fell in June and broke my ankle, Don was a big help to me. He came over and taught me how to walk on my crutches and even helped me take care of the kids. His mother would come over and help me with the house and laundry during this time. My children and I were happier than we ever had been.

After I got my cast off, I started going to an old doctor in the West End area. He told me my foot would be OK but I was too fat and seemed to be depressed. The only thing that seemed really strange about his diagnosis was that I only weighed 125 pounds and was really pretty happy for a change. He gave me two prescriptions and said they would help me get back in shape. I didn't know until a few months later that he had given me diet pills and Valium.[1]

This was in April 1970. I never was a big eater, but every time I took the pill I was supposed to take a half hour before I ate, I would feel sick to my stomach and couldn't eat at all. When I called him about it, he said I was supposed to take four a day of the other pills that he had given me, too. Since I hadn't taken any of them yet, I thought it would probably help. They were marked "Valium, 5 milligrams," but that didn't mean anything to me, as I had never heard of them before. After I started taking these along with the ones I later learned were diet pills, I began to lose weight rapidly and cried because I was hungry all the time and couldn't eat hardly anything at all. I got to where I couldn't sleep at all either and I was having trouble walking. I would be walking across the floor and just pass out cold.

I had a different worker by now. Miss Engles was very nice, too, and since she and Miss Moore were roommates I was not a stranger to her. I told her I was seeing a doctor and taking medicine he prescribed. She was very concerned about my loss in weight and my appearance in general, so she decided to send me a homemaker for another week to see if being able to stay in bed, along with the medicine, might be helpful. I know now that this homemaker was really a blessing in disguise. She was a retired nurse's aide, and after just two days of being with us she asked to see the medicine I was taking. When she looked at the prescriptions, she told me what was wrong with me. When I told her thanks and I wouldn't take the pills anymore, she said that it wouldn't be that easy to just quit without proper help. She told me that City Hospital had a very good drug program and would be able to help me, but I would probably have to spend some time in the hospital.

When I called my stepsister at last to see if she would keep the kids, she refused and said I was not only a tramp, but now I was a drug addict. The next day she called the church and told them about the drugs and also that little Kathy was a bastard. She told them that since Don was a decent boy, they should keep him away from me and help her to take my kids away from me. This really hurt me very much as I really liked Don and none of my new friends knew anything about my baby.

By this time I was also losing track of time and couldn't concentrate on anything long. I also lost my memory quite often. One thing my stepsister didn't count on was that the church would help me and my kids instead of her. On May 2, 1970, they called Miss Engles at the welfare and told her I had to go in the hospital. The only problem they had was I didn't want to go. Miss Engles told them she agreed I had to go but understood why I didn't want to. She told them she would come out and make me go herself. Believe it or not, this was the first time I ever told anyone about being in Chatwood. However, at this point I didn't have any choice. She said she would sign me in City Hospital herself to try to prevent me from going back to Chatwood. She also said that way I couldn't leave the hospital until I got well.

My stepsister was there, too, along with a couple of ladies from the church. When Miss Engles asked her to keep my kids, she said she wasn't going to keep my kids while I ran the streets like a tramp. When Miss Engles told her to shut up, she got angry and left. The other two ladies from church asked Miss Engles if they would be allowed to keep my children under the circumstances. She told them yes, and we both thanked them very much. I loved the children and told them good-bye. I still didn't want to go, but I realized I couldn't take care of the kids in my condition. I knew Miss Engles was trying to help us, so I agreed to go. By the time I got to City Hospital, on top of being sick already and the shock of leaving my kids, I couldn't talk or respond at all. All I could see was the nightmare of Chatwood happening all over again. I guess Miss Engles told them I had been in Chatwood before. They told her no matter who signed the papers that as soon as Chatwood got a bed available that they were sending me there anyway.

When I heard this, whatever I could have communicated with them was totally gone. They agreed to keep me on 9 North [the psychiatric ward] until they could get a bed at Chatwood. I remember hearing people talk to me, but I just laid there in a half-conscious state. I was so sick and frightened that I couldn't even drink water. There was a very nice nurse who worked at night. After the third day on 9 North, she said if I would try to drink or eat I might get well, but if I didn't they would have to give me IVs, since by now I only weighed 98 pounds. She also told me that she and the other staff on 9 North were fighting to keep me from being sent back to Chatwood but I had to fight, too. After about an hour, I did manage with her help to get down a glass of ice water. She was very happy after I drank the water, and I even managed to say hello. She went to the doctor and told him that I deserved a chance to stay on 9 North for a while anyway. He was so amazed that I had finally responded to some-one that he agreed. After several weeks I was able to walk and talk again and even began to eat some. I still had the loss of memory, but somehow that didn't seem important anymore.

After seven weeks, I got to go home for 10 days. At this time, Kirk was three years old, and Kathy was nine months. I was far from feeling strong yet and the kids were a lot to handle. Ten days later I ended up back in the emergency room at the wel-fare's request.

This time City Hospital was full, so they sent me to Tanner Psychiatric Institute. This was on July 10, 1972. I had to stay in Tanner until October 28, 1970. However, Miss Engles and Miss Moore came to visit me weekly and even brought the kids to see me. This really did help my recovery.

Tanner agreed to release me if I would follow through on their referral to the West End Clinic, where there was a mental health worker. One reason for the referral was because of medicine. When I was in City Hospital they had me on a new drug called Navane. When I went to Tanner, however, they had changed me to Mellaril. Since I had to have medicine they told me that the clinic also had a very good psychiatrist available every week. I really wanted to go home and agreed to follow through on the referral.

I went home on October 28th. The welfare brought Kirk home at this time because he was older. The lady from church still had Kathy. This really bothered me, however, because it seemed as though nobody understood that I loved my baby, too, and wasn't getting to keep her at all. She was a year old now. I still cooperated with them in every way I could, because I loved both my kids and wanted to stay well enough to raise them.

On November 10, 1970, I met Doctor Bergmann for the first time. When I met him, I couldn't believe he was a doctor at all. He was very polite and made me feel like he really cared about people. All the time I was in City Hospital and Tanner I had never got to talk to my doctors at all, and by now I wanted to find out what my problem was and if I would ever get complete-ly well again.

When I asked Dr. Bergmann this, he smiled and said he cer-tainly had hopes I would. He said he didn't know yet what the problem was, since the hospital records weren't very clear. I did continue seeing him and Sarah Johnston, who was the mental health worker at the clinic, on a regular basis. I really respected Dr. Bergmann and felt if I would ever get well that he was the one who would help me accomplish it.

Sarah and I worked well together, too. When she and Dr. Bergmann felt I should have little Kathy home, too, the welfare agreed. We all three were at last a happy and whole family again.

Everything went well for the children and me until 1971. After I got a regular schedule with Sarah and Dr. Bergmann, I began to feel better. Dr. Bergmann had changed my medicine again; this time he put me on Elavil.

The last of November I decided to get a baby-sitter and start working again. One of the reasons for this decision was the fact that I felt like my kids and I had been caught up in the web called "the system." I was beginning to feel I didn't have the right to control our own lives anymore. I had no problem finding a job since I had a good work record. I went to work at a dime store downtown. I felt very proud being self-supporting again. Since the clinic had evening hours, I could still continue my counseling.

In March 1971, we were told to move because they were going to tear down the building we lived in. Kirk had just turned four in December, and Kathy was almost two by now. This made it hard to find another place to live. I finally got an apartment on the second floor of another house. This was on Miller Avenue in the West End. We moved on April 1, 1971. That same month Kathy became very ill once again. I took a leave of absence from work and carried her to the clinic every day for two weeks. We lived close to a mile away, and since I wasn't working I didn't have bus fare for all of us to ride. The last day I had to take her I got sick and passed out just as we walked in. I made an appointment for myself the next day. The doctor ran tests on me then and told me a week later that I had rheumatic fever. She told me I could take penicillin and stay in bed at home and see her regularly. This sounded fine, except with two babies and no one to help me, it was impossible. However, two weeks later I had no choice when she called welfare and wrote orders for a homemaker and made me quit working. I not only was very sick physically, but I had a feeling of failing and being right back where I started from. When the welfare decided I should go back to City Hospital for both physical problems and depression, my medical doctor agreed.

The lady who baby sat for me kept the children. When I got to City Hospital, they sent me up to 9 North. When I told them about my medical problems and that I needed my medicine, they told me I couldn't possibly have rheumatic fever at 27 years old, and I had to take what medicine they gave me. I was upset, since the medical doctor had explained to me that although it was rare at my age, there was no doubt about my having it. Since she had been treating me for about two months now, I asked them to call her. They told me my doctor there would have to do that the next day. That night, even though I took the medicine they gave me, I couldn't sleep. When I went in an empty reading room to read, a man told me to wait there and he would be back soon. I didn't know he was the nurse until he returned with two other men and put me in restraints and seclusion for being up late.

The next day the doctor I had there called the clinic and had to admit my medical problems were real. He started me back on the medicine I had gotten from the clinic. I also told him I had been seeing Dr. Bergmann before I became ill and couldn't get in to see him. I told him about taking the Elavil and that it helped me to sleep at night. He said he didn't feel my problem was depression and put me on Trilafon. Since most of this hospitalization was spent in restraints and seclusion because they felt I wasn't trying to cooperate with them, I was glad it only lasted 10 days. I knew the problem was not all my lack of cooperation, but rather a total lack of communication all the way around. I really couldn't tell them how I felt myself. I know I'm not easy to deal with when I'm sick, but this type of handling from their end only made it harder for me to say how I felt. It frightens me and makes me feel like they aren't listening anyway. I was really glad when I got home and went back to see Dr. Bergmann.

Dr. Bergmann never treated me bad and always tried to help me sort out what I was feeling. I only told him I was in City Hospital again and that they changed my medicines to Trilafon. He did change the medicine back to the Elavil, since it seemed to help me more. I finally recovered physically and went back to work.

Everything seemed to be going well when Kirk started kindergarten in 1971. I was still seeing Sarah and Dr. Bergmann at the clinic and was attending a parent-training class for behavior modification to help me be a better parent. I don't recall exactly what was happening when Sarah felt I needed to go back in City Hospital in 1972 for a week or 10 days. When I told her I didn't want to go in the hospital anymore, she said she would talk to Dr. Bergmann and make the decision for me. Since we had gotten along pretty well, I didn't argue with her.

Note

1. The doctor who prescribed inappropriate medication for Rose was incompetent. He left town when a child died as a result of medication he had prescribed.

The Nightmare
of Depression

8

Once again I was on 9 North. Once again I spent another two weeks feeling like nobody understood me anymore, including myself. Sarah had placed the kids in the Children's Receiving Center. She took me to City Hospital. I was there a month.

When I came home, Sarah began talking to me about adopting out both my kids. When she almost had me convinced I should, I talked with Miss Moore about it. She felt after all I had been through for my children that to adopt them out would be tragic for all three of us. She did suggest placing them in foster homes for a year so I could concentrate on myself for a while.

Later, in June of 1972, after two more short hospitalizations on 9 North, I was doing well and had even started working for the city at the West End Neighborhood Services. My ex-husband had decided to marry again, and he and my stepsister decided to take Kirk away from me after six years. I tried to kill myself and ended up back in City Hospital.

In August 1972, still in City Hospital on 9 North, I talked to Miss Moore and Sarah and gave welfare temporary custody of the children for a year so I could try to get well and we wouldn't be torn apart all the time. I loved my kids with all my heart and wanted to do the best thing for them. The only thing the hospital and I did agree on was the love I had for my kids and my constant struggle to get well and be a good mother.

Dr. Bergmann and Sarah were working at the Central Community Health Board at this time, too. After three weeks, City Hospital felt they could release me if I would attend the day-treatment center there. I often wonder what our lives would have been by now if I hadn't kept up with Dr. Bergmann. He didn't know anything about my giving temporary custody of the kids to welfare. It was becoming obvious to me that Sarah wasn't being totally honest with me or him. When he found out that I had signed the papers for the children, he told me, as my doctor, to never sign anything again when I was sick. He also said never to make any decisions that important during these times. I really liked him and respected him more than anyone I ever knew. To this very day, I still follow the advice he gave me then.

Miss Moore then told me she couldn't keep our case any longer because she was too emotionally involved. This was early 1973, when the case went to the Children's Protective Services.

During this time in City Hospital, my stepsister told City Hospital that I had beaten Kirk on the head before I left. Since I couldn't seem to remember anything during all my episodes, the hospital and I checked out her report. Even though I had been sick often, I had never abused the children in any way. When City Hospital found the report to be a lie, they sent welfare a letter saying they had had me as a patient at least six times in two years, and that although I was stubborn at times, they had never known me to be violent. I then learned that this incident is what got the Children's Protective Services involved. I still felt that to give us all a year was for the best.

I started attending day care after my release. I also let welfare place the kids in a licensed foster home in order to prevent Elton or my family from bothering the children. Little did I know that welfare's real motive was to keep me from seeing my children unless I cooperated with their demands. By now I was getting sick of the word cooperating. It never ceases to amaze me what a mother's love for her children can do.

Since the children were still at my baby-sitter's house, I was asked to take them myself to the new home in Silver Hills. I talked to both children about my decision. They were seven and four now. Since I never lied to my kids or made any promises I couldn't keep, they always trusted me completely. I reminded them to always remember their prayers and be good. I followed the worker's car with the kids in mine. We sang on the way to keep from crying. After we got to Mrs. Smith's [the foster mother] house and I asked about visiting, I was told that Mrs. Smith did not own the home. I was told to ask Mrs. Betz [another social worker assigned to this new foster home]. Mrs. Betz told me that I could see them every two weeks from 1 P.M. to 5 P.M. after she checked with Sarah to be sure I hadn't missed any days at the center for my rehabilitation.

Since I had agreed to see Sarah and attend day care willingly, this idea made me feel more like I was being forced to go instead. I did attend regularly, however, and I benefited from the program and graduated.

During this time, my visits with the children were cut even more and I was denied the right to correct them at all when I had them. At the age my children were and the fact that they were very normal as well, their hearing another adult tell me I couldn't correct them regardless of how they acted made things impossible.

Two weeks later, when Kirk, age seven now, decided he wasn't going back to Mrs. Smith's after our visit, Mrs. Betz had made it clear to me that I must have the children back on time or I would be charged with kidnapping my kids. When it was time to leave, Kirk began kicking me and yelling. Since my time was running out, I called Mrs. Smith. Mrs. Smith agreed Kirk needed a spanking, but if I gave him one, she knew Mrs. Betz would follow through on her threat to seek permanent custody. She told me to let her call Mrs. Betz at home.

About 15 minutes later Mrs. Betz called me. She told me not to touch him but to put him on the phone. She told Kirk if he would be good and go back, she would take him out the next day for an ice cream. Believe it or not, she did just that. I called her and told her I was angry with the way the whole situation was handled, that she had only rewarded him for his bad behavior. The only answer she had was that since I was crazy, my children had to be, too.

When I turned to Sarah about this, she told me she had talked to welfare and she was convinced I wasn't best for my children either. Since I had always trusted Sarah, I couldn't believe she was really saying this. I told her I refused to trust her or cooperate with her any longer. I then made an appointment to see Dr. Bergmann myself. He was the only person in the world that I still had any trust in at all. The only thing I said to him concerning Sarah was that I felt I needed more help than she could offer me then. I was really surprised when he said he had felt the same a year ago, but he didn't feel I would have accepted his saying so then. I did agree to continue seeing Sarah less and seeing Dr. Bergmann more often.

On December 23, 1973, Mrs. Smith called me and said if I didn't come after my brats, she would kill them. I didn't know what was going on, but I went straight to her home. When I got there, she was gone. Her son, Bob, told me she had taken all four kids out to eat. He said his mother was mentally sick and had to give up all four of the foster children. When I told him I couldn't take the kids without Mrs. Betz's permission, he said to call the Children's Receiving Center and they would have her call me.

When Mrs. Betz called she started yelling and cussing because I was there. When I tried to tell her what was happening, she wouldn't listen. She just yelled at me to shut up and don't take the children anywhere.

She never knew that when Mrs. Smith came back I not only took Kirk and Kathy but also the other children and Mrs. Smith to my house for the weekend. Since I had lost my job and our home the year before when I became ill, I was living in a one-room apartment on Clinton. It was rough that weekend with so little room. By Sunday Mrs. Smith was OK enough that I could take them all back to her house.

The following Friday the welfare brought my children home, bag and baggage. They said that Mrs. Smith was sick, and they didn't have another home open. They said they couldn't take me to court since my actions with them were voluntary and they couldn't find any evidence of abuse. They told me as long as I agreed to continue working with them voluntarily that no court would ever give them a commitment on the children unless there was real evidence of abuse. What they were really saying, in fact, was I really didn't have any choice.

Since the apartment I had was government housing, I had to wait for a larger apartment. I wasn't getting ADC and only got $82 from general relief. When Mrs. Betz began threatening to take the children again unless I got a place with more room, I became very upset. Then she called the owner of the building and demanded that he move us immediately. They told her it wasn't that easy. I was really caught in the middle since I was told by welfare that I couldn't get ADC until I moved to a larger apartment, and I couldn't find anything on $82 per month income either.

The Nightmare of Depression

Two weeks later, Mrs. Betz came to my home and gave me one week to move or lose my kids again. I told her she wasn't being fair to me at all. I also told her that she never intended to help any of us in our own home but only wanted some evidence for court. She not only didn't deny what I said but seemed proud of it. She even said they knew if they put enough pressure on me I would break. She told me that if I ever had to be hospitalized again, for any reason, that would be evidence enough. I didn't know why I got sick, but I knew I honestly couldn't help it.

She then called the landlord again from my phone. During the conversation, I heard her say that "Rose wouldn't mind that." When she hung up, she told me they had an apartment and I could keep my kids. The new apartment was on West Becker and Milford. Just the looks of the neighborhood itself were frightening. I then learned that Mrs. Betz's remark on the phone had meant that I didn't mind moving into an all-black apartment building.

When I met the lady upstairs, she asked me why I put my children in this position. I had to admit that I wasn't even aware of it. She could tell I was serious, and we became very good friends. Since she had five kids, she was a big help with getting Kirk settled in school. When I moved to the new apartment, Mrs. Betz told me she was giving my case to a Martha Jones, who was a supervisor and would know how to handle me better than her. I really felt that in the Children's Protective Services I had been handled more than enough. It seemed like all I did was try to cooperate with everyone and nobody other than Dr. Bergmann seemed to listen or try to cooperate with me.

When I met Martha Jones, she really scared me. She told me plain that they had been after a permanent commitment all along. She said everyone had to have weaknesses in character and she was determined to find mine.

This was in November 1973. When Kirk got sick in January, he appeared to have the three-day measles. I always kept both children in the clinic for their health care. I kept him home and in a darkened room for three days. After the three days, he didn't have any fever or rash, so I sent him back to school. The next morning he woke up with his eyes swollen shut and couldn't see at all. I took him to the clinic that day. The doctor said that although he seemed to have the measles, it was scarlet fever instead. She suggested taking him to an eye specialist to care for the swelling and loss of sight.

I really felt awful about this. I felt like I should have been able to prevent it. I called a specialist the following day and got an appointment. When Martha Jones came that afternoon, she said I had to cancel the appointment and take him to her doctor. I knew she felt I had harmed him in some way. I knew better but I didn't argue, since my only concern was getting him to a doctor. Kirk's eyesight did not completely return for almost three months. I talked to the school and was allowed to give him his work orally at home.

By the time of my birthday in June, Kirk was fine and had passed to the second grade. Miss Jones had never let up all this time. Between her constant harassment and the ordeal with little Kirk, I was sick again. This time my fear of losing my kids because of being hospitalized again was more than I could handle. Miss Jones said she could also take them if I stayed home in that condition. I had nothing to live for anyway.

I overdosed on the Elavil. I don't really know what happened then, but somehow I got to Dr. Bergmann. He told Miss Jones that if she got someone to help me at home, he thought he could help me without putting me in the hospital. I couldn't remember taking the pills, but I think when Miss Jones realized what she had done, she called Dr. Bergmann herself and agreed to help me.

Since the welfare's involvement was also indirectly putting both Dr. Bergmann and me in a position of avoiding any hospitalizations, he decided to try the Haldol injections at the daycare center. As I said before, I don't remember much except that by the end of the day I was allowed to go to Mrs. Smith's house with my kids for the weekend. She had recovered pretty well and had kept up with me and the kids. By Sunday night Dr. Bergmann let me go back to my own house. He wanted me to start the daycare program again. I had to admit the Haldol treatment had worked like a miracle.

Although Dr. Bergmann said he couldn't promise me I would never have to go in the hospital again, we at least felt with the Haldol I certainly had a good chance of preventing it. He said that the Haldol itself was not new, but only the method of rapid tranquilization. The method that day had worked so amazingly well on me that it was really unbelievable. I was so confused when I went, I didn't know if it were day or night and I thought the world had already ended. I was afraid of everyone, including Dr. Bergmann, whom I had never been afraid of before.

The Nightmare of Depression

By the end of the day I knew who I was and where I was and recognized some of the people around me. I was still very frightened and didn't say much, but I had certainly regained my trust in Dr. Bergmann.

When I told him the next week what had led up to this episode and what welfare was doing, it explained some of the fears and feelings I had while I was ill. I didn't remember overdosing at this time, which I feel probably caused the end-of-the-world thoughts I had.

Another thing which caused this feeling was that a few weeks earlier Dr. Bergmann and Sarah had requested Miss Jones to terminate her case with me because they felt I had too many people pulling me in too many different ways, which was only worsening my condition.

Miss Jones brought a paper out about two weeks before I got sick stating what I just said. However, she told me that if I agreed with Dr. Bergmann and Sarah and signed the paper, no matter what happened to me or my children again, the welfare would never help us with anything, including our ADC and food stamps. She also said that if I didn't sign it within 10 days, it would automatically be signed anyway. I never signed that paper, but it was signed over a year later.[1]

I then agreed to make a videotape with Dr. Katz and Dr. Bergmann at the medical center of City Hospital. This tape was on the results of the Haldol method helping patients whose very world depended on avoiding hospital stays. It also covered the events with welfare that had led to this illness. This was made in the fall of 1974.

Note

1. Dr. Bergmann had written a letter to Miss Jones stating that some of Rose's problems were caused by too many people in the welfare system telling her what to do. Miss Jones took offense at this and wanted Rose to sign a retraction that Miss Jones had written at the bottom of the letter. Rose would not sign. Miss Jones then threatened to withdraw welfare assistance, food stamps, and ADC. Rose does not know who signed the letter.

New Home—
Kathy Becomes
the Victim

9

On June 6, 1974, I moved to Sycamore Street in Silver Hills. When we moved to Silver Hills we had the nicest apartment we had ever had. Kirk was seven years old and Kathy was almost five.

I had to drop out of counseling, since we lived out of the Central Community Health Board area, where I saw Sarah. I did continue to see Dr. Bergmann at City Hospital every month or two and got my medicine from him.

After I moved, Miss Jones decided to turn me over to a new worker. She made such a big deal over the change that she insisted on taking me out to lunch with the new worker and with Sarah to say good-bye to her and Mary [a social worker].

During the illness I had before we moved, Miss Jones had placed Kathy in the Washington Day-Care Center so I could go to day care myself. After we moved, she said I had to continue taking Kathy every day no matter what. Since I didn't have a car, this was pretty hard. Kirk started school two blocks away from home at 8:15 A.M., and I had to have Kathy downtown at 8:00 every day. The only way I could work it out was to take Kirk on two buses to take Kathy to day care. Then we had to take two buses back to his school and get there by 8:15. We had to do the same thing at night.

After I took Kirk to school, I had to continue on two more buses to day care myself, since I still had about three more months before I graduated. After I left the health board at 1:00 P.M., I would get home about 3:00 and start out to collect the kids. It was no wonder I became physically ill by October. Since we had all gone to the 10th Street Clinic, I made an appointment for myself after dropping Kathy off.

The doctor there was very concerned and had me come in daily for blood work and other tests. After a week she said she had to put me in the hospital. I was under so much pressure that I got hysterical, and they were holding me because I was crying and trying to hurry to take Kathy to day care before she was late. They had someone take Kathy for me and insisted I tell the clinic worker what was going on. I didn't talk to the worker about anything except that I was going to day care and they would help me when I got there.

After I calmed down, they took me to the day-care center. They did give me a couple of shots of Haldol that day. I didn't tell my day-care counselor I was physically sick, but I did tell her I couldn't keep up this pace any longer. She agreed that it was too much for anyone, and I graduated a week later. I never went back to the clinic either. I was really physically sick. I was in so much pain in my stomach and I had a lot of trouble breathing.

I continued taking both kids to school until Christmas. A day before school was out, Kathy developed impetigo all around her mouth. I kept her home and used medicine and kept cleaning it. As I was doctoring her mouth, I asked her if she had been putting crayons or anything dirty in her mouth. She started crying and said she was afraid to go back to school. I finally got her comforted enough to tell me why. She told me one of the men who worked as a janitor there had put his worm in her mouth and the dirty stuff from it was choking her, and she couldn't wash it all off.

Since she was barely five years old, I knew she wasn't lying. I just had to recover from the shock enough to decide how to handle it. I told her she didn't have to go back no matter what the welfare said.

I called Kathy's doctor and took her to the hospital. I called the day-care center and reported the incident to them. I also called the protective services worker the same day. I can't believe that that worker really refused to believe my child because I had a history of mental illness. Kathy was taking a nap, so I decided to clean while I was thinking of what to do next. About twenty minutes later the police were at my door. They asked me if I called about a rape, so I told them I did not call them, but I did have one to report. The officer called the welfare worker right then and told her I had the right to think things out and to call them myself.

Since the janitor's little boy and Kathy were the only white kids at the center, it wasn't hard for the police to pick him up. I was so angry and upset all I thought of that night was hurting him myself. However, I knew this wasn't right to even think about. So I called Dr. Bergmann and talked to him. I told him I was going to prosecute the man, but I didn't really know how to go about it and I was concerned about my angry feelings. Dr. Bergmann said the feelings were normal but to stay with the law and the court and he would help us both.

It was early December when the grand jury indicted him. However, it was April before the trial actually came to be heard. This was very difficult for little Kathy and me since it had taken me two months just to get her to sleep without me again and to begin to return to her normal self. During these four months, I never mentioned the trial to her but only comforted her when she would have a nightmare or become frightened. I was really amazed at how clear her memory still was by the day of the trial and the prosecutor talked to her.

I was also very thankful when Dr. Bergmann came to the courthouse that day to be with us during the trial. His being there meant a lot to both of us, since after only five minutes I couldn't stand being in the courtroom and had to sit in the hall. Kathy did an excellent job with the lady officer handling the case. The case was lost on the fact that the man had threatened to fold her up in her cot and take her away if she told on him. There was little doubt that he was guilty, but believe it or not, he was freed on the fact that the cots did not fold up but stacked on top of each other.

When it was over, Dr. Bergmann told me that I had done all anyone could do under the circumstances, and the only thing left was to hope that since Kathy was so young that in time she would forget about it. It is really understandable why so many rape cases are not reported.

After I finished day care in November 1974, I didn't see any counselors and didn't know if there were any available in the Silver Hills area. After the children's protective services worker had refused to testify as a character witness for Kathy at the officer's request, I told her that if they did not close my case and stop harassing me that I would seek the services of a lawyer to put an end to their interference with my family.

Then this same worker, Silvia Thomas, came out the next day and demanded I put Kathy in another day-care center where she would be the first white child to enter the school. I was so angry with her that I told her just what I thought about her and the protective services department. I also told her that if she did not leave immediately, I would call the District Three police station and have her removed from my home. When I finally picked up the phone, she left. Two days later, she mailed a form for me to sign closing our case.

Two people from the day-care center did go to court for Kathy. One lady was a social worker for the center. Her name was Barbara Baker. During the trial and afterwards, Barbara and I became very good friends. We talked a lot about what careers we had always wanted most. I told her my dream had always been to go to college and become a good social worker so I could help people who had had problems and experiences similar to mine. She said she thought I would be very good at helping other people and that I had done a beautiful job helping little Kathy through her experience without her needing professional counseling.

Barbara arranged for me to get a government grant and get started at Central City University. This was in the fall of 1975. In September I started at CCU. Barbara's dream also came true. She moved to Texas to take up modeling.

I really loved going to college and made pretty fair grades. I had problems getting a dependable sitter, finding time to do my work with a six- and eight-year-old at home, and no transportation. I even ended up hitchhiking during the bus strike that winter. I still didn't give up until March 1976, when I was studying for my final exams and Kirk set his bedroom on fire playing with matches.

What really made me quit, besides the mess I had to clean up, was that Kirk said he deliberately started the fire because he wanted to kill me. I had a serious talk with him as to what would make him feel like that. Although I really felt he was just saying this so I wouldn't punish him, I hadn't spent as much time with him since I had started going to CCU.

Since he wouldn't really tell me why and he sounded so serious about his desire, I felt he might need some counseling himself. I took him to the Psychiatric Services Clinic at City Hospital. I was surprised when, on the day of our appointment, he was not only ready but even excited about going. I knew he had just turned nine, but I was really becoming more concerned about the little guy. In all my life I had never seen anyone so happy about going to see a psychiatrist.

When I learned why he was so relieved about going that day I was so shocked I didn't know what to say to him. I knew that Kirk had been acting out with the baby-sitter and telling her wild stories about people trying to pick him up on his way home. When the sitter and I talked about these incidents, we just thought it was his age and imagination. I don't know what he said to the doctor that day, but he told the sitter and me that night that when he was answering the phone at night while I studied, someone had been calling and saying that they were going to kidnap him and Kathy after school to hurt me.

After he told us this, we decided for her to stay and answer the phone that evening. The real shock came when she answered the phone that evening and we learned he was telling the truth. After three calls, I decided to answer it myself. When I heard the same threats I called District Three police station. They talked to the phone company the next day and put a tracer on our line. I kept a record of these calls and a week later the phone company only told me the number they were traced to. They also warned the party of the penalties for this.

When they told me the number, it certainly answered all my questions about phone calls over the last nine years. The number belonged to my stepsister, Debra. When she called, as herself, later, I told her I knew everything, and I have never spoken to her since.

I quit college, and Kirk only had to have one more appointment at the clinic. Our lives finally got back to normal

While the kids were at camp, I was redoing Kirk's bedroom wall and became poisoned from the dust from sanding the plaster. I became so ill that when I went to City Hospital emergency I had lost so much oxygen from my system that they told me later I had complete heart failure. However, they did a beautiful job of bringing me out of it. I had to hire the rest of the work done.

Depression Again

10

I was seeing Dr. Katz and making videotapes with him after I got out of college. I did not see Dr. Bergmann while I was making these tapes. I was having some problems dealing with the feelings these tapes were bringing out. Since I had no one to talk to about these feelings, and only got to talk to Dr. Katz on camera, I told him I needed to talk to him without the cameras and tape.

He didn't agree to this and I ended up on 9 North in City Hospital again in August 1976. When I had been there a few days, the nurse told me that Dr. Katz had scheduled a taping for the next day for me. I was so upset and confused that I knew I could not handle the session at all. When I requested for the only time in my life to be secluded, the staff decided to talk to Dr. Katz themselves. They did seclude me, since it was obvious that I was very upset and confused.

A week later we did have the taping session, since he agreed to see me later himself. Afterwards, we agreed to postpone the taping until after the holidays. I never saw him alone or at all until January 1977.

The children and I were doing fine as a family since the welfare was no longer involved, and I had completely broken all contact with my stepsister and her mother. Over the holidays, I thought I would like to try to see if I could handle working. Since St. Anne's was nearby, someone suggested I contact them. All I really knew about them was that they had helped us at Christmas a couple times. I decided to go and see if they could use some help.

That was when I met Doris Wagner. She was very pleased with the idea and said I could start in February. I worked in the front office answering the phone and filing. I really enjoyed the work, and Doris was very pleased with my work and often told me so. After three weeks I was volunteering 40 hours a week. The kids were really happy with my job, too, since they could come to the office after school and eat cookies while they did their homework. We were very happy.

There were two things which caused our final disaster as a family, and began 18 months of heartbreak and sorrow for us all. One was the tapes I had been making again. One tape was on the conditions at Chatwood in the 1950s when I was there as a child. This tape brought back many memories that I hadn't allowed myself to think about for years. I had a private session with Dr. Katz in February. I told him I was having nightmares and was feeling suicidal as well.

He said that he felt the cause of these episodes was that as a very small child, even before I went to Chatwood, I was very intelligent. To survive I had taught myself to totally block out anything that was too painful to remember or deal with. One example he used was my excellent grades and records in school. He said that to cope with the many changes and losses or abuse in these homes, my only outlet was to concentrate on my school work completely and try to pretend the other things were not there.

He also said that that was was probably the reason I had been able to adjust so well in society after what I had experienced at Chatwood. He said that I had learned to block things out so well that I had begun to block out everything, including the time of day and the present time, which sent me into a state of total confusion.

He said he knew I really couldn't control what was happening, but that in time, if I could force myself to talk about the things that happened, and deal with them, I could accept what had happened and forget it.

I told him the only thing that I couldn't understand about what he said was the fact that I had never had an episode in my life until after my daughter was born in 1969. He then said that he wasn't aware of this and had assumed the episodes were the reason I had been in Chatwood. He then asked me when and where my daughter was born and how soon afterward the first episode began. After I told him, he said that we would not make any more tapes until after he talked with Dr. Bergmann.

When I went home I was still feeling suicidal, but I thought maybe if I tried what he had suggested about talking to someone about my feelings it might help. The only problem I had was that I hadn't seen a counselor in three years and didn't know where to look in the area. When I went to work the next day, I decided to ask Doris Wagner what services were available in our area. She said she was a counselor herself and would be happy to give me some time. I was a little uncomfortable with this idea since I also worked there full time. However, since she was also my supervisor, she said nobody would know the difference.

I talked to her the best I could about what had been happening and what I was feeling. To make things worse, a week later I got a call from a Phil Schwartz at the Children's Protective Services. He said he was my new worker and would be out the following day. I told him my case was closed and they were not supposed to bother me anymore. He said he had just taken over and mine was the only case on his file that the welfare had never got any kind of commitment on the children.

I have to give him credit for being determined. He showed up the next day. When I answered the door, he walked right in, showing me his picture I.D., and sat down saying he was not leaving until the kids came home. He began talking nonstop about them never having a commitment on my children. I said it was because I had worked with them voluntarily and would he please leave? He not only refused to leave but informed me that the police would not remove him as long as he was doing his job politely.

Since it was obvious I wasn't feeling well, his being there really bothered me. He said he knew I was sick again and did I have a counselor? I told him I was seeing a worker at St. Anne's. He demanded to know who the worker was. I told him it was Doris Wagner. I was surprised when he said she was a good friend of his, and they had gone to school together. This also bothered me, since I had been trusting Doris as a counselor. When he wanted her phone number to call her about me, I told him I should have someone I could confide in who would not talk to them. I also told him I was doing volunteer work there and that nobody in the office knew that Doris was seeing me professionally. He promised he wouldn't bother me at work if I would give him her number. After I gave him her number, he finally left. This was in March 1977.

I had been going downhill ever since February anyway, and now with the welfare suddenly appearing again, I was getting worse. I was also afraid to turn to Doris now as well. Two days later Phil called the office. Since I was the receptionist, I naturally answered the phone. He wanted to talk to Doris. All the workers were in a staff meeting until noon, and I had orders not to interrupt them except for emergencies. When I tried to explain this to him, he told me to put her on the phone or he would go downtown to get a commitment on the kids that day. I didn't know what to do.

The youth counselor had come in. Since we were friends, I asked her what to do. She told me to give her his number and she would get Doris herself, even if she did get angry. Doris did leave the meeting to call him. She made an appointment to see him with me on Friday. Doris had promised to take me to lunch and shopping for the board dinner that Wednesday. She had been very pleased with my work and had told me when there was an opening she would consider hiring me for pay.

The next day was March 23, 1977. It was the last day I worked at St. Anne's. That afternoon I was so confused I couldn't remember how to answer the phones. Then Phil walked in, showing his I.D. to everyone in sight and demanding to see Doris and me right then. Since Doris was off that day, I went home. They told me I did go to the board dinner on the 24th but was afraid of everyone, so they took me home. I don't remember anything that happened for the next week until they took me into the quiet room at a psychiatric center. The only thing I remember while I was in the quiet room was being in severe pain. I not only had a severe headache, I was laying on the floor and my arms and legs were hurting so bad it felt as though they were being twisted and pulled in different directions at the same time. Every time I would come to enough to tell them, they would give me another shot and I would go back to sleep. When I came to at last, I was really frightened because I didn't have any idea where I was or how I got there. When I realized I couldn't get out because the door was locked, I sat down and tried to remember what happened and where I might be. No matter how hard I tried, I couldn't remember anything. When I tried to walk around the room, I could only take a few steps without falling.

Depression Again

Finally Dr. Lawson came in and asked me how I was feeling. I told him about the pain and that I still had trouble walking. He said that was why they had put me in there, so I wouldn't fall and get hurt. When I asked him where I was and what happened to me, he said I was in the Tanner Institute, but he was hoping I could tell him what had happened and how I got there. He said I came in from City Hospital on the 27th, that I couldn't walk or talk to anyone. He said the only information City Hospital had given them was that I had been brought in to them as a psychiatric emergency by a worker from St. Anne's. Since I couldn't remember anything, Dr. Lawson and I could only work on getting me well enough for us to find out.

After a week, I had recovered from everything except the amnesia. I did remember my kids, though, but didn't know where they were. That was when I met Donald Miller, who was my social worker there. He was very nice. Since I couldn't remember, he decided to call St. Anne's and talk to Doris. He said since she had been the one who took me to the hospital that she must know why, and also where my kids were.

After he talked to her, he said he still wasn't sure what happened to me, but I had lost my kids to welfare. He said they were in the Children's Receiving Center and the welfare was going to file for a permanent commitment to adopt them out. He said Doris was coming to see him and did I feel we could trust her to help? At this point, I didn't know how I felt about Doris or anyone else. I did realize, however, that Doris was the only one who had any idea what was going on.

On May 12th, I went to court with Mr. Miller and Mrs. Furlong, one of the nurses at Children's Hospital who had become very involved in the case. Doris went with us as well.

The Trial

11

I wasn't allowed to see my children since we had parted in March, and was only allowed to talk to them for five minutes on the phone for Mother's Day. Doris was the only person whom Phil would allow to visit with or talk to the kids. I had hoped they would be at the courthouse for the trial, but they weren't. The case was thrown out of court that day because of lack of evidence and the way it had been written up by the welfare. I thought then I would be able to go home and get the children. When welfare told Mr. Miller that they were going to refile immediately, I didn't even get to go home.

Doris had been acting strange all day. When we got back to the hospital, she took Mr. Miller aside. Later, she came upstairs to see me. She was crying. She told me that until that day she didn't know if she really wanted to help me. She told me the truth about what really happened. She said she and Phil had been friends for a long time and that she let him convince her I wasn't a good mother for my children. She told me she had never seen anyone as ill as I was that day at St. Anne's and thought that I was pretending in order to get her attention. She said the two youth counselors, Jane and Mark, who had brought me home from the dinner decided to come down and see about me and the kids the next day. When they saw how sick I was then, they called her to come down.

Since this was the same day we had made the appointment with Phil, he showed up later, too. Doris said I was slumped in a chair and talking out of my head. When she tried to talk to me, I couldn't. She said I didn't seem to understand anything. She didn't understand why I was being so stubborn with her when Phil was sitting there, too. She said she even tried yelling at me and threatening to shake me, but I just didn't respond to anything.

Jane finally told her she knew I wasn't being stubborn but was definitely having some kind of breakdown. When Doris finally agreed I should go to a hospital, Jane asked to keep the kids herself. Phil then lied to Doris and said that nobody could keep them because he already had a commitment. Doris then let him have the kids and took me to City Hospital.

After she told me the truth, she was still crying. She asked me to forgive her and let her help me get them back. She said she would prove to me I could trust her if I'd give her another chance. She was really sincere in what she was saying. I couldn't believe what happened because I had always admired her. I know it's hard to believe, but even after everything that had happened, there was still something about Doris I liked. I did give her another chance. I'm really thankful now I did.

I still had to stay in Tanner Institute until the next hearing. When Dr. Lawson heard that I had been seeing Dr. Bergmann all these years, he was pleased. He felt if anyone could give me encouragement at this time, Dr. Bergmann could.

When he located Dr. Bergmann he was working at Chatwood, right across the grounds. After Dr. Lawson talked to him, he said he hadn't known anything about all of this. I then began seeing Dr. Bermann every week while I was still in Tanner.

The next trial was scheduled for August 6th. Everyone concerned felt I would have a better chance of winning if I wasn't in the hospital. I was released on August 1st.

When we had had the first hearing in June, the lawyer I had then felt the outcome of the trial would depend very much on my being able to remember what had happened to me. This bothered me a great deal, so while still at Tanner I felt if I could go home it might help me to remember easier. When I couldn't get a pass, I ran away and came home to try to remember. When I got home, the house was a mess, with the kids' toys scattered around, clean laundry on the couch, and dirty dishes in the kitchen.

As I sat down and tried to remember, I started crying because I thought about what Dr. Katz had said to me about the cause of the episodes. However, I realized that I could remember anything, regardless of how painful it was, in order to regain my children, the only thing I had ever had to live for in my life. When I still could not remember anything, I lost faith in Dr. Katz's theory completely.

When I went back to the hospital, I talked to Dr. Lawson about this. Dr. Lawson was the first one to ever mention to me that he strongly believed these episodes might very well have a medical cause. He also said that since I had an early history of being in Chatwood, whenever I got in these situations, it was automatically assumed that I was a mental case. He then asked me if he could do some testing on me.

He had a complete skull series and EEG done, as well as complete psychological testing. The strange thing is that with all the hospitalizations, this was the first time I had ever been tested psychologically. Since Dr. Lawson was leaving for Phoenix, I later learned the results of these tests and his theory through a letter he had written for my trial.

The results showed that I had suffered minimal brain damage at some point in my life and that I still had a problem with motor-graphic coordination, particularly on the left side. Although the psychological tests found me to be quite intelligent, during most of these episodes I had problems with my speech, loss of memory, and a total lack of concentration. Also, the constant threat of losing my children definitely brought on suicidal feelings.

If there was anything humorous about this whole trial, it was the fact that I was being tried for mental illness for not being fit to care for my own children, yet they were throwing medical and psychiatric questions at me that probably some of the most educated doctors could not have answered.

I had gotten a Legal Aid lawyer before the August 6th trial. Her name was Cynthia Chandler. I really liked Cynthia from the first time I met her. She was very young and very bright. She was also very determined to help me get my children back.

By the day of the trial, she had at least 13 witnesses for me, including Doris and Jane from St. Anne's, Mr. Miller and Mrs. Furlong from Tanner, and Dr. Bergmann. The others included my landlady, a schoolteacher of Kathy's, and a man from the Board of Education whom I didn't know. The children were at the courthouse as well.

I know if I live to be a hundred I'll never forget that day. Other than my divorce and the trial with Kathy, I had never been to court. I felt so bad and was so nervous about the outcome of the day that I don't know what was holding me up. I knew my witnesses would be there and I expected the welfare department and my children as well. However, I was surprised to see my ex-husband and his sons there. We had not heard from Elton in almost two years.

When I saw a gray-haired lady talking to Kirk, I asked my lawyer who she was. I nearly passed out when she looked at me and said, "Rose, don't you know your own sister [Julia]?" When she realized I hadn't seen her in nearly 20 years, Cynthia was concerned and asked that all witnesses and unconcerned parties remain outside the courtroom during the trial.

Elton was inside the courtroom since he had a lawyer and was asking for the children, too. When Elton's lawyer asked me why I would not let him have his own children, under the circumstances, I told him that we had not heard from Elton for two years and that only Kirk was his child.

When Elton's lawyer realized I was telling the truth, not only about the children's fathers but also that I had never neglected or abused them, even during my illnesses, in the closing arguments he remarked to the court that he had never seen anyone prosecuted simply because they had no family backup or support, and that I should have custody of my children.

The trial lasted six and a half hours. Welfare had asked for a permanent commitment and adoption, which would mean I would never see or know where my children were again. As I sat waiting for the judge to decide, Cynthia said she could get Dr. Bergmann if I needed him. I remember telling her that if they got the verdict they asked for, that even as good as Dr. Bergmann had been, I doubted even he could bring me out of this one. She said not to give up, because she could always appeal it.

They did not get the permanent commitment they had asked for, but they did get a six-month temporary commitment. We were all glad at first, because we thought that in six months, if I did well and agreed to see Doris on a weekly basis and continued seeing Dr. Bergmann every week as well, things would work out all right.

What really made me happy was that the court said I could see my kids every week. Since I had only got to see them three times since April, this meant a lot to all three of us.

When we found out that Phil had been making plans to place the children in the Willow Creek Home until they turned

18 and to use the six months' commitment for the next 11 years, Cynthia and I decided to appeal the decision (see Appendix for Court of Appeals decision). Since Kathy was only seven, they would not take her at Willow Creek, and Phil asked me to let them go to St. Francis, since it was a lot nicer than the Children's Receiving Center and they could only stay at the center for three months anyway.

After I let him move the children, he decided to give them to my sister, Julia, and her husband. The very thought of this terrified me. Since I had never told anyone how Julia had abused and mistreated me as a child, I knew I had to now since my own children were in danger. I told Doris and Cynthia about the abuse and my concern for the kids.

When we got a hearing, they were only interested in Julia now. Even when Annette, my other sister, tried to tell the court how miserable Julia had made her own children's lives, the court still granted Julia custody of my kids.

After the hearing, I tried to tell Phil about Julia in hopes that he might understand. Instead of understanding, he decided to personally supervise my visits with my kids at the orphanage to make sure I didn't say anything against Julia, because he wanted my kids to love her. He supervised my visits completely. After a month, I began to feel like I was visiting three kids instead of two. When the kids and I went for a walk, he went, too. If we played a game, he had to play, too. The only real problem Phil had was when Kathy wanted me to take her to the restroom and he couldn't go, too.

I will never forget the first time I took her and we were alone. She hugged me and started crying. She said, "Mommy, I know you love us and you always taught us to say our prayers, because God loves us, too, and helps us." When she looked at me and asked why God didn't listen to her prayer before the trial and let her come home, I told her that God did love us and he would help us when he was ready, that just because he doesn't always do what we want right away doesn't mean he isn't listening. She stopped crying then and said she would keep praying.

This was September of 1977. In November of 1977 the kids went to Julia's house in Green County. I had missed two visits with the kids in October because I had pneumonia. I was not allowed to see the kids on Thanksgiving because welfare wanted them to adjust with Julia. I was really depressed with the whole situation.

By this time, Doris had become concerned about my mental health because I had not really shown any emotions or expressed any feeling in all these months. She said she had asked Ruth Atwood [a social worker] to go to all the court hearings with us in case I let go of all the feelings I was holding inside. I really don't know why, but even though the trial took 18 months, I never let go of the feelings I had. One reason may have been because I was feeling so many things at once, I wasn't even sure where to start.

When I didn't get to see the kids that Christmas season, Ruth invited me to go downtown with her and her 10-year-old daughter to see the decorations and eat lunch. Since she knew I always took my kids every year, she thought it might help me through the holidays. I did go with her and really enjoyed her little girl.

Although Doris and Ruth were a big help to me, I still felt more trust and confidence talking to Dr. Bergmann. I told him on one of my visits that he was the only person I knew whom I trusted enough to even go see at Chatwood. Until I started seeing him there, I had never been near the place in all those years. Although I saw him there for over a year, I never walked through those gates but what I had some awful feelings or memories of some kind. What made it even harder was that his office was in the same building I had been in as a child. With all these feelings from the past added to the feelings and memories I had of Julia and knowing she had my own kids in her hands, I think I was afraid to even try to express any feelings to anyone.

I know Cynthia has to be the most sincere and patient lawyer anyone ever met. During the 18 months, we got more surprises and unexpected people showing up from my past.

When Elton had the story put in the newspaper, the welfare got calls from people wanting to adopt the kids. Some of these people even offered to take all three of us. When we finally won the appeal in September of 1978, the newspaper reporters were waiting for the verdict, too. When Cynthia asked me about letting the papers have the story and the verdict, I told her I didn't want the publicity and that the children and I were going to have to continue to live where we were. She agreed with me that we should be able to live our lives in privacy and that even today most people don't have very good ideas about mental illness.

After the trial was over and the children came home, I had a party for Cynthia's success and a welcome home for the kids. Everyone who testified for us, including Dr. Bergmann and the two witnesses from Tanner, showed up for the party. Although Ruth did not testify, I invited her because she did attend all the hearings and stayed with me in the courtroom. We all had a wonderful time that day and we all certainly had earned the celebration.

The next week I went to see Doris and she told me she couldn't counsel me any longer because she was too emotionally attached to me. She said she wanted me to stay with the agency and work with Ruth. I was very upset about losing Doris, and although I had never said anything even when I worked there, I had never especially liked Ruth. However, I did realize that I was very attached to Doris. Since she had done so much to help me get my life back, I agreed to see Ruth.

The first time I went to see her, she told me that my only problem was that until I met Doris no one in my life had ever put any controls on me for anything I did. She said that although I looked up to Dr. Bergmann and respected him, he was not doing me justice because he was too overprotective of me and he never put any controls on me in all the years I had known him.

I told her I had never given him any reason to, and unless I was seriously ill, I always listened to him. I also told her that when I was really ill that anybody could lead me anywhere if I trusted them. I also told her that I had more controls put on me in my life than anyone I knew.

When she said she was going to use controls on me whether I liked it or not, I couldn't help but ask just what she had in mind. The only answer she gave me was that I would find out when the time came. I never went back to see her for over three months since I got really sick on Christmas Eve that year.

It was the first Christmas the kids and I had had together in two years. I didn't enjoy it since I had 104-degree fever all day. During Christmas and New Year's I went to the emergency room twice and got medicine. Even with the medicine, I still got sicker and couldn't break the fever. I hadn't been to a medical doctor since 1974, except when I had pneumonia and went to St. George's emergency room.

By January 3, 1979, I finally gave up and called the Silver Hill Clinic. I met Dr. Babcock. I was not only sick, but I was really scared because the kids had only been home two months. I knew I couldn't go in the hospital. I wasn't just sick and scared, I was also trying to avoid telling Dr. Babcock what I was afraid of. She finally told me that whatever I told her was confidential and that whatever a person is dealing with mentally can certainly affect them physically as well. When I told her everything that had been going on, she understood how I felt since she was not only a doctor but a mother as well. I not only got better soon with her medical care, but I really learned to trust her.

I kept in touch with Dr. Bergmann by phone during this time. I told him the children and I were having a lot of trouble adjusting to each other again and I felt we all needed some type of family counseling. I told him I wasn't working with Doris any longer and that Dr. Babcock had told me about the Mental Health East Clinic.

He said he knew them well and worked in the evenings there sometimes. He said he would see about getting me an appointment. When I didn't hear from Mental Health East or Dr. Bergmann, I thought they were probably too busy to take us, and I decided to go back to Ruth. I knew that Dr. Bergmann had left Chatwood, but we had lost contact.

I continued to see Ruth over the summer, and in September of 1981 I finally got in touch with Dr. Bergmann. He had lost my phone number when he changed offices. When his secretary had called St. Anne's they wouldn't give her my number because I was a client. Ruth had forgotten to give me a message to call him.

In September, Kathy had a serious bike accident at the park. When Kirk and Kathy came in, Kathy was bleeding through her clothes from her privates. Both kids were as pale as ghosts and Kathy fell in my lap. From the way they both looked, I really didn't want to ask what happened. The phone rang and I found out she had ridden a ten-speed bike into a wall and run the handlebar in her. A friend had called to offer to take her to the hospital.

Although Kathy was only 10, she weighed close to 90 pounds. I'm still not sure how I picked her up and carried her upstairs and out to the car. I took her to the hospital, where they got her patched up. When I started having back pains only two days later, I thought it was because I had carried her. When I saw Ruth on Wednesday, everyone noticed I was limping. I hadn't noticed the limp, but I knew my back and legs were still hurting.

I saw Dr. Babcock the next day and she thought maybe I had pulled a disc in my back. She sent me to get an X-ray. The X-ray was fine, but I sure wasn't. By the next Wednesday, I couldn't walk right at all and was in a lot of pain. I had gone back to City Hospital twice that week at Dr. Babcock's request. I got some pain medicine and muscle relaxers from them.

The Trial

When the emergency room at City Hospital didn't find out what was wrong with me, Dr. Babcock asked me if I trusted her enough to go through City's main clinic as her patient, since she worked there. I told her I didn't trust anyone that much.

Because I had had such a hard time at City Hospital during Kathy's birth and the many psychiatric stays, I was not anxious to be anyone's patient there again. She understood how I felt and asked me to see Dr. Johnson, who was a friend of hers and a neurologist. I called Dr. Johnson's office and got an appointment for two weeks later. During this time, my legs had drawn up so much that when I walked it almost looked as though I was sitting.

Since I couldn't get in to see Ruth, she wanted to come to my house to see me. I knew I was very sick and felt terrible. However, when Ruth came down she was angry with me because she thought I was psychosomatic and the doctor just wouldn't tell me so. I told her I didn't know what the word meant or why she was angry. She told me to find somebody to keep my kids and I better call Dr. Bergmann to help me understand what my illness was. When I lost the use of my left arm completely a few days later, I ended up with Dr. Johnson and in Memorial Hospital. I had sent my kids to stay with a friend of mine in Murray Hills.

The two weeks I spent in the hospital were not any easier for my doctors than they were for me, since nobody really knew any family medical history. Ruth insisted that I call her every day, but she refused to see me or talk to my doctors. I was really frightened and wasn't even sure if I was going to make it or not. I was really hurt by the way Ruth was treating me when I needed her the most. On top of being sick, she had made me feel as though I had done something really bad to be in the condition I was. I had kept in touch with Dr. Bergmann. He was a big help to me emotionally. When I finally told him and Dr. Johnson what Ruth said was wrong with me, they had a hard time trying to convince me that she was totally wrong.

When I came home two weeks later, I was better but was still weak and had trouble walking. After I got home I started having problems with two women who lived in my building. I knew I couldn't turn to Ruth with this problem and I was too weak and sick to protect myself. After only six days at home, I ended up in City Hospital emergency suffering from shock. After they brought me out of shock, they sent me to psychiatry and to Tanner. After I came home and talked to Dr. Bergmann, he insisted I let him make an appointment for me with a worker at Mental Health East. He also said he was sorry he hadn't done it before when I had asked him to.

It was October 1981 when I met Diane Duffy. By the time I got to Mental Health East, Ruth had me so mixed up and convinced that I was going to be put away for good if I didn't straighten up that I was really afraid to give Diane a chance. I asked her if I could go back to St. Anne's.

I was really hurt when St. Anne's refused to take me back. However, I'm really thankful now they didn't. It took me a good six months to begin to settle down enough to work with Diane. I have really come a long way in the last six months and trust her more than any worker I've ever had. I know I still have a long way to go and it won't always be easy, but I really feel that by the time I leave Diane, if I can ever be mentally well again, I will be.

December 30, 1985

12

I have been in counseling with Diane for five years now. The prognosis for complete recovery in the next few years looks great. When I left off, I was only seeing Diane. However, a few months later she introduced another therapist into our sessions. Her name is Ellen Davis. At first I did not like Ellen, as she was new to me and very good at bringing out things that are very hard for me to handle. One reason for this is that she is not only highly trained, but works mostly with children. This turned out to be a real blessing because there were a lot of problems that started in my childhood that I couldn't remember. At first, I resented not only her, but Diane as well. I am happy and proud of the progress I have made and the many discoveries and hard times the three of us have overcome in the last three or four years.

I am still seeing Dr. Bergmann, and he is happy with my progress. Although I always looked to him and trusted him, what I really needed in my life was a good, decent woman I could learn to love and trust as well. I know this was the hardest part of my treatment. I not only started trusting Diane, but even learned to love her as the mother I never had. Ellen picked up on these feelings when we realized that every time Diane would get sick or go on vacation, all kinds of things would happen to me.

The first time she left, I had a car accident and broke two ribs. Since she was gone, I called Ellen. She took me to the hospital and helped me through it all. That was when I had another scary thought. I realized that Ellen really cared about me, too, and that I not only loved and trusted Diane, but I was really learning to trust and like Ellen as well.

The second time Diane left me, I developed shingles and suffered severely for almost three months. I still made it in to see Ellen, who was very supportive to me. After Diane returned, she explained to me that my illness occurred because I was suppressing a lot of feelings deep inside. They both felt that whenever I felt abandoned or was afraid of losing someone close to me, I began to suffer physically because I couldn't express how I felt and at times did not even recognize my feelings.

When she left for vacation, I had a major crisis as well as a major breakthrough in my therapy. I suffered so much physically that I ended up needing exploratory surgery and an appendectomy for my psychosomatic symptoms. While I was in the hospital, Ellen came to see me and talked to me by telephone often. When Diane returned, she and Ellen brought me home and came twice a week to see me while I was recovering. I began writing about how I always ran a fever and became ill on Friday as a child when I knew I had to go home for a weekend visit and did not want to go.

After my surgery, I began having very strange and horrible nightmares. One night, while lying in bed, I saw and felt the presence of a little girl ghost. For about three days I had some strange experiences with this. Since I am a sensible person who doesn't even believe in ghosts, I began looking at it in a psychological way and realized that the little girl was only my way of bringing out my fears and feelings from childhood.

About two weeks after my surgery and my ghost experience, Diane told me she was going to leave for surgery. It was on a Tuesday. She hugged me good-bye. Although I had hugged her many times, this time I felt her fear about having surgery. That evening I got a headache and couldn't sleep all night, even with medication. I kept saying, "I know Diane is never going to come back." In the morning, I knew I would need help mentally. Since Ellen would not be in until 9:00 A.M., I decided to take a shower and collect my thoughts, so I could tell her exactly what I had gone through all night. While taking my shower, I got a severe headache and became dizzy. I then realized that all these things that had been haunting me for years were not imaginary, but were actually real memories from my past. While letting my mind drift and trying to remember, a horrible thing happened.

December 30, 1985

The water running over me from the shower appeared to be blood, and I had a helpless urge to stab myself. I finally managed to cry, which broke the trance I seemed to be under. I called Ellen immediately and she took me to the emergency room. Because she and Diane knew I had always feared restraints in the hospital, she sent me to the crisis center, which has 24-hour care but does not use physical restraints or harsh ways to deal with people. I had told Ellen on the way to the hospital that I remembered having shock treatments as a child and what was wrong with me was remembering, which would block out the present time. She said she believed me, but that we had to keep me safe until we could sort it out.

She came every day to see me and we put together a very horrible reality from my past. With Ellen's help I remembered being in Chatwood State Hospital at age 10, even before I was probated a year later. I remembered being on an adult ward and becoming very close to a young girl of 19 who protected me. I loved her like a mother. I remembered her killing herself in the bathtub and dying in my arms as I helplessly watched her blood going down the drain.

Since I was only 10, I did not understand much about life, much less death. Ellen and I felt the recent anaesthetic and the sleeping medication at the center had all helped in this discovery, as well as with the connection I had made between the fear I felt about Diane and the fear I felt about the young girl who died in my arms so many years ago. Diane is the first woman I have loved or trusted since the young girl. It began to make sense why I would fear losing Diane so much. It also became more apparent that when I became ill after my daughter was born, each time I faced the hospital I became ill again because I was afraid I would lose my children, whom I loved very much. The most frustrating part of all this is the lack of records to verify that I spent almost a year in Chatwood before I was even probated. I also know that at one point while there I was stabbed and received blood transfusions. Although the records have been destroyed, as are all records over 10 years old, we know from hospital tests in 1979 that I definitely had had blood transfusions in the past, which caused me to have toxic hepatitis. Trying to prove all of this is really frustrating and can make a person very angry when you are either told a record has been de-stroyed or that you don't have a right to see it because you were a minor at the time.

Rose's Story

After every road I tried seemed to lead to a dead end, Diane suggested I confront my dad and stepmother, as they always had control over my life and placements during childhood. This turned out to be more interesting than I thought. Before I called my dad, I decided to make him believe we already knew what I wanted him to tell me. It was a real surprise when he admitted I was in the hospital a year before I was probated. But he claimed it was City Hospital to test my mind and that he and my stepmother visited me every week for months. Then I asked him why I could remember as far back at four years old but couldn't remember that whole year? He then told me to ask my doctors. I told him I knew I had had shock treatments and blood transfusions. At first he tried to play dumb. Then I told him I knew the truth about my stepmother being a housekeeper for him and my real mother and her stealing him from my mother. This I really could prove from records and was not bluffing about. He then shouted that if my doctors or anyone had any of these records, there would be the biggest lawsuit ever seen, as he had had all my records sealed permanently. Then I realized that he would have had to sign for everything so he had to know the truth. But he never told me, as he died three weeks later from a heart attack.

That was when I met my real brother, the youngest of the three boys. He and I had hardly seen each other in 27 years but were glad to find each other. Since I had been going to the courthouse and other places and finding documents that could help prove my past memories, I trusted him and his wife with it all. Since then, my brother, sister-in-law, and I have proved so much that I no longer doubt my own sanity. We have proved how my stepmother along with my dad altered records for years to cover up my stepmother's evil deeds and the marriage she ruined. We also learned there was a seventh child born after my real mother and Dad divorced. Since I was the last child my real mother had, that only leaves my stepmother and Dad as the parents.

I also got to meet my real mother two weeks ago. I had been taught to hate her and told she was a tramp, alcoholic, and declared unfit to raise us. She is now in a nursing home because she has a pacemaker and can't live alone. Otherwise she is very mentally strong for age 76 and has a personality so beautiful for all the hard times she has had. People have often said the same about me. Finally getting to meet her was wonderful. I am so much like my mother that it was just like sitting on my couch and watching and hearing myself talk. I told her I had always hated her because a child who has never been with a parent can only know what others tell them about that person. I asked her to tell me her side of the story.

I am writing her side now as it is only fair to a woman who went through every avenue available to her at the time to keep and raise her six children. Since this story began 41 years ago, we must remember that laws were very different and welfare programs and jobs, especially for women, were limited.

Between the two years after my youngest brother's birth and my birth, my mother had a miscarriage. She didn't regain much strength before becoming pregnant with me. During her illness before her pregnancy with me, my dad moved in the lady who is now my stepmother to care for the other five children and the house. Shortly after my mother became pregnant with me, she caught the two of them sleeping together. Because she was ill, pregnant, and still loved my dad, she would not get a divorce until after my birth. My dad and stepmother moved out to live together, leaving her alone with five children and ready to have me. She and I both spent over two months in the hospital after I was born. She was very ill and had what they called a milk-leg [thrombosis of a vein]. I was born with pneumonia. When she came home, Dad was still gone and the house and kids a mess, so the welfare gave her carfare to juvenile court where she filed for a divorce. She walked the streets with all six kids, looking for an apartment because of an eviction notice. When she could not find an apartment or her husband, she took us all down to the police station and filed nonsupport charges and got enough help to keep us with her until they found our dad. They found him over in [state] living as man and wife with my stepmother. Then they brought him back to Central City and put him in jail for not supporting his kids. While waiting for the hearing, my mother got news that my stepmother had come to Central City and put up bail and that they both had left again. Finally the eviction came. All her belongings were in the street on December 14th, 1943. When she finally found my dad, he came with my stepmother to get the furniture and us kids. They cleaned us up and had us taken to the Children's Receiving Center.

My mother, while still very ill, asked a Greyhound bus driver to let her ride to Wisconsin, where her family was. She said they would pay the bus fare. He not only let her ride but bought her the first hot meal she had had in a long time. It took her a long time to gain back her strength, but slowly she did. She got a job in a cannery, hoping to earn enough to come back and raise her children. Just as her dream was about to happen, she became ill again. Still she didn't give up. She met a man who offered to marry her, bring her back, and help her raise her children. She thought after she married him her dream would come true. I don't know how she withstood all this heartache, but after three weeks, her husband left her stranded. She then read an ad asking for a lady to keep house for a widower in Central City. She saw hope in this ad, not only for a job, but for a chance to see her children while she worked. When she wrote him a letter, she told him she didn't have any money to come back. He sent her a bus ticket and she came to work for him. She had her own two little rooms to live in while taking care of the house for him.

Her dream was crushed again when the welfare allowed her to see us. I was eight years old then. My dad and stepmother had her visiting rights denied, saying she was unfit to see us since she was living in the house of a man to whom she wasn't married. Over the years, they have twisted everything to make her look unfit and make my stepmother a saint. Four years later this man built a brand-new home and asked my mother to marry him so they could live together. He married her in October 1957, and they moved in together. In November, exactly one month later, he had a heart attack and died, leaving her crushed again.

I am not writing this just to make my dad and stepmother look bad, but they truly were by making me hate a mother whose only fault was truly loving her husband and children. My brother, sister-in-law, and I have found many legal papers to prove her story, even to exact dates. The sad part of this is the fact that we can never forget the lies they told us or get back the 41 years without her. But we can love her for the time she has left.

I have made a lot of progress in the last year with the help of Diane and Ellen. I think the hardest thing to handle was having to accept just how much my dad and stepmother really hated me and destroyed my life to cover up their own guilt. My brother and his wife are still supporting me and helping me find documents and living people to help bring back my memory so I can deal with all this better. My therapy is a really big help as well. It is not easy to accept what you remember when you can't get records to help you. I even got so frustrated that I asked Dr. Bergmann if I could have sodium pentothal treatments to bring back my memory. He told me he did not have much faith in that treatment, especially for things that happened so many years ago, and that it might bring me more pain and suffering. He allowed me a consultation with a specialist, who agreed that I did not need anything that would bring me more pain and suffering. I have decided to keep trying to get records and put together what I do remember during therapy.

Now that I realize why I got sick when Diane left me, I have not gotten sick this time, and she has been gone six weeks on family business. I am really looking forward to the future, since I have made several great accomplishments in the last few years. I went back to college two years ago and tried to get a degree in social work and psychology. I was making all A's, but had to quit because I could not keep up the pace, and they only offer grants for full time or nothing. This really broke my heart, but maybe someday they will have home courses I can afford and I will try again. I even went back to work doing phone sales for three months this year. I did well, but became ill with too much pressure.

I know I have a lot of common sense as well as a lot of intelligence. I also know there's a way out of this system I've been caught in for years. I really believe if I keep praying, working with my therapy, and progress like I have been, I will find my way out. I have great hope for my own children. Kirk is 18 now and wants to join the Marines when he graduates. Kathy is 15 and making the honor roll. Her dream is to become a police officer. My dream is to get well first, find a decent, loving husband, and become self-supporting again. I know with all the people helping me, my dreams are close and I can make them happen.

Epilogue

At 38 years of age, Rose made another attempt to become self-supporting. She took a job as a telecommunications operator, but a few months later she suffered a near-fatal heart attack. Rose underwent surgery to correct a congenital heart defect that restricted the supply of blood to her heart.

After undergoing bypass surgery, Rose made a remarkable recovery. Her depressions have not recurred.

When asked why she thought no physician had ever suspected a heart condition, her response was one of resignation: "They always thought I was nuts because I had been at Chatwood." Thus a troubling question remains: Can a diagnosis of mental illness blind social workers and/or medical personnel to the possibility of underlying physical impairment?"

Perhaps a thorough physical examination should be required within the first six months of a person's receiving welfare benefits. Rose's story clearly illustrates how the loss of human potential and hundreds of thousands of taxpayers' dollars might have been avoided with a thousand dollars of modern medical tests.

With her health restored and spirits high, Rose started a new job search, eventually taking a part-time job as clerk in a service station convenience store. Her health history made it difficult for her to find a full-time job that provided health insurance benefits because prospective employers did not wish to assume the additional insurance costs.

After several months of successful part-time employment, Rose began to have trouble with her legs and feet. The vein transplantion during heart surgery caused poor circulation in her legs. Because her job required hours of standing, she had to quit.

Rose is a fighter, a survivor of the first order. She had one alternative left. She needed more money for herself and Kathy. Rose's disability allotment from Social Security was very small, and the welfare allotment for Kathy would end when Kathy turned 18 in the near future.

Rose began to investigate the possibility of receiving income from her recently deceased father's railroad employee's pension plan. Her persistence paid off. After months of personal effort and the kind help of an attorney, Rose qualified for payments as a daughter with a life-long handicap. She now receives double the amount she was receiving from Social Security Supplementary Income. Again, one wonders why the welfare department never investigated the possibility of Rose receiving compensation from an outside source.

A happy event must be reported. Rose bought a pair of new eyeglasses—a direct result of her improved financial status. She was diagnosed as legally blind several years ago and declared unable to drive a car. But an optician found a lens that gave her 20/20 vision in her good eye. She had no vision in her other eye as a result of the eye problems she suffered as a child. Her new glasses arrived during the Christmas season. She was ecstatic and proclaimed her restored vision the best Christmas present she had ever received. Again, with all of the health care services Rose received during her life, why had no one attempted to correct her vision problems?

In this story of tragedy and human error, Rose has found a measure of personal reward and happiness. Rose's daughter, Kathy, a high school honor student, joined a police-cadet program for teenagers. Well-liked by the officers, Kathy asked her police friends to keep watch while her mother locked up the gas station at midnight. Although Rose did not know it at the time, a police officer in a "taxi cab" parked near the gas station was watching over her. Kathy is the child Rose refused to abort and fought the courts to keep. Kirk, Kathy's brother, is now on his own and self-supporting.

Betty Nafziger

Appendix

Cynthia Chandler filed Rose's case with the Court of Appeals, citing that the judgment of the county court contradicted the manifest weight of the evidence and that it contained several errors. The Court of Appeals decision went beyond the interests of Rose and her children in that it set new guidelines for determining when a lower court should remove children from their natural parents and give custody to an agency. In its decision, the court focused on the "care of the children" rather than on the "emotional or mental health of the parent." If children are not subjected to neglect or abuse, if their behavior and school performance are satisfactory, and if the parent has been conscientious in making care arrangements for the children's care, mental health should not be a determinative issue in granting custody. The following was drawn from the appellate court's decision:

> The psychiatrist, who had treated the mother since 1973 on a periodic basis, diagnosed her problems as recurrent episodic depressions, but he saw no reason why she could not be a competent mother. The depressions will recur, but with less frequency; she is not likely to deteriorate and has matured as a human being. The doctor reported, as did other witnesses, that one cause of her depressions was the stress she felt from pressure exerted on her about her children by the Welfare Department. The children are the focus of her life, and the . . . threat or even suggestions of removal of the children brought on debilitating reactions. In fact, she was kept in the hospital for an extended time after the instant complaint was filed in order to assist her in setting down and preparing herself for appearance in the Juvenile Division hearing. The Welfare Department did not rebut the clear suggestion that, in recent months, it had exacerbated the situation, unknowingly

111

but inevitably; there is a paucity of evidence demonstrating any attempts to cure and resolve a difficult situation.

Militating in favor of a finding of dependency is the evidence about those periods of time when the children had to be placed immediately with someone else when the mother was hospitalized, and the many moves from one residential location to another. The mother managed to make some provision for the children each time, but she was nonetheless physically unable to care for them while in the hospital. While the children have apparently experienced a normal development, they have had problems with adjustment in the past and are subject to wide, perhaps irrational, shifts of attitude. They appeared, to one Welfare Department worker, to be scared and nervous during at least one of the mother's depressive episodes.

In this case, we find none of the instability and impoverished conditions of the mother's life, none of the failure to support or care for the children, and none of the psychological dependency and affectionate attachment of the children for foster parents or others standing in loco parentis. . . . (70 OApp 2d 123 [Ohio 1980]).